MIRACLE AT METLAKATLA

MIRACLE AT
METLAKATLA

The Inspiring Story of
William Duncan, a Missionary

Written by Margaret Poynter
Illustrated by James Padgett

Publishing House
St. Louis

Concordia Publishing House, St. Louis, Missouri
Copyright © 1978 Concordia Publishing House

MANUFACTURED IN THE UNITED STATES OF AMERICA

Library of Congress Cataloging in Publication Data

Poynter, Margaret.
    Miracle at Metlakatla.

    (Christian heroes)
    SUMMARY: A biography of the Christian missionary who helped the Tsimshian Indians
establish a new home in Alaska.
    1. Tsimshian Indians—Missions. 2. Duncan, William, 1832-1918. 3. Metlakatla, Alaska—
History.   4. Metlakatla,   B.   C.—History.   5. Missionaries—British   Columbia—Biography.
6. Missionaries—England—Biography. (1. Duncan, William, 1832-1918. 2. Missionaries. 3.
Tsimshian Indians. 4. Indians of North America) I. Title. II. Series.
E99.T8D856   266'.023'0924 (B) (92)   77-29125
ISBN 0-570-07876-8
ISBN 0-570-07881-4 pbk.

To my grandmother, Helen Stevens.
She loved Alaska and all of its people.

Contents

Prolog

Why would a young man leave the comfort, warmth, and security of his family to travel to a wilderness peopled by what were said to be bloodthirsty savages?

Many people asked this question when William Duncan left England to make the journey to western Canada in 1857. There were certainly many reasons why he should stay home. William had a promising future in the business world. He would probably never lack for money or material things. He could enjoy music, literature, and drama. He had many friends and a family who loved him.

If he went to Canada, he would face disease, primitive living conditions, and lack of money. He would also be living among the Tsimshian Indians, who were said to be heathenish, ignorant, and brutal. Other missionaries had tried to preach the Gospel to these wild people. They had had little success. There was no obvious reason why William should do any better than they had.

Well-meaning men spoke words of warning to William. The only words he heard, however, were the ones spoken one rainy night at a missionary meeting. At that time God had called him to work among the Tsimshians.

William went to western Canada. Fearfully at first, then boldly, he told the Indians about Jesus. The Indians listened. Their first suspicions were natural enough. For years the only white men they had known had cheated, oppressed, and misled them. White leaders had given them "hooch," which dulled their senses and kept them submissive. The Indians were uneducated, confused, and completely dependent upon the Hudson's Bay Company.

By cutting through red tape and exposing hypocrisy, William quickly made enemies among his own race. Some of his most outspoken enemies were members of his own church. In the end it was the white man who turned out to be William's greatest challenge. The Indians had become his supporters, his friends, and his family. When he had to leave Canada to escape persecution, they followed him.

William Duncan was fully 100 years ahead of his time in his fight for equal education, social equality, and human rights. He stood apart from most churchmen of his day in his realization that along with spiritual nourishment men need food for their bodies and work for their hands.

The real miracle at Metlakatla was the demonstration of what can be done when people work together, hold uncompromising principles, and put their faith in the Lord.■

1

William Makes His Decision

William Duncan stood straight and tall as the older man shouted at him.

"Why, the very idea is preposterous! If I should allow you to go to Port Simpson, it would be the same as to sign your death warrant. The Hudson's Bay Company cannot undertake to be at all responsible for your safety. You are only 24 years old. I certainly don't want to be a party to your murder."

"But, sir, I'm determined to . . ."

The officer continued as if William had not said anything. "Why not remain here at Victoria? We have several thousand Indians right here who need a missionary. If you want to work among them, I'll see to it that you get all the help you need."

"The problem is that I was sent to Port Simpson, and that is where I must go," said William. "Even if the Missionary Society were to change my orders, I want to go to Port Simpson."

"Young man," continued the official, "I know the situation there. You wouldn't last three months among those savages."

"I must go," repeated William. "All I ask is that you let me stay here long enough to learn the Tsimshian language. After that, I'll take full responsibility for whatever happens."

The older man sighed and shook his head in defeat. "Well, if you are bound to be killed and eaten, I suppose that is your business. We will just have to let you go."

William felt like shouting for joy. If this man had not given him permission to continue his journey, the dreams and plans he had made for over a year would have been shattered.

William Duncan's dreams had actually started four years earlier, in December of 1853 in Yorkshire, England. It had been a dreary, stormy night, and he had felt like staying home instead of attending a missionary meeting at St. John's Chapel. A book and a roaring fire looked much better to him than a long walk in the rain. Then at the last minute he shrugged and decided to go. After all, he had promised to be there.

He was soaked to the skin when he arrived at the church. Not surprisingly, there were only a few others in attendance. As he sat in one of the front pews, he rubbed his hands together and tried to forget how cold he was. He couldn't help overhearing the mumbled conversation of the vicar and the guest speaker as they stood nearby.

"I think we should call the meeting off," whispered the vicar. "There are only about 30 people here."

William wondered if he had come all this way for nothing.

"No, no," answered the speaker. "If they came out in this weather, they deserve to hear a message."

William settled back as the rector began to speak. Before the talk was over, he had forgotten about his wet clothes and his chilled feet. Nothing mattered except the words he was hearing. It was almost as if they were directed right at him.

The rector was concluding his talk. "Missionary workers are desperately needed in foreign fields. Are there any among you who can answer this call?"

William left the meeting without speaking to anyone. He walked home slowly, not feeling the driving rain or the slush beneath his feet.

Why shouldn't I become a missionary? he thought. Isn't it possible the Lord has work for me to do in heathen lands?

On the other hand he had a good job, a comfortable home, friends and relatives here in England. His mother—what would she say about his running off to uncivilized parts of the world? Was it really fair to cause her to worry?

He frowned. The decision was not a simple one. He had always gone to church, sang in the choir, played the organ, and helped in whatever way he could. Wasn't that enough?

No matter what arguments he came up with against being a missionary, he could not rid himself of the feeling that he had received a call. He decided to talk it over with the vicar as soon as possible.

The following day as he made his rounds as a salesman, his thoughts were on unknown shores, dark jungles, and the thousands of people who were waiting to hear the Word of God. As soon as he was through with his work, he went to see Vicar Carr.

Without any hesitation he blurted the words out, "Vicar Carr, I want to become a foreign missionary."

The vicar leaned back in his chair and smiled. "It is strange, William. Do you know that I prayed for the Lord to put into your heart the desire to devote your life to this very work? You would be very wrong to ignore this call."

William sat down weakly. He had been right. This was not just a foolish idea. "I knew it," he said humbly. "The feeling was so strong I couldn't ignore it."

William found it hard to concentrate on the prayer. I have to tell my employer—and mother—and all my friends. It has all happened so fast. O Lord, give me the strength and conviction to see this through.

When he told his employer of his plans, the older man stared at him in disbelief. "But you are our star salesman," he said. "You have a great career ahead of you."

"All I know is that I must go," said William. "Nothing can change my mind."

"Are you unhappy here? If it's the money, I am prepared to offer you a partnership with a handsome raise in salary. What would you make as a missionary—perhaps 150 pounds a year?"

"Thank you for your offer, sir," said William, "but I have made up my mind. It's not the job—I have been very happy here."

"To throw yourself away like that, when I know that you have one of the most brilliant business careers in England before you." His employer pounded on the desk. "Don't you know that you are making a fool of yourself?"

When William said nothing, the older man sighed. "Well, do one thing for me anyway. Stay with me for six months so I can train someone to take your place."

William felt that he owed him that much, so he agreed.

William felt as if the six months would never pass, but he was grateful for the time. At first his mother had pleaded with him to change his mind, but as the weeks passed she had slowly accepted the idea. He was also able to say proper good-byes to his friends and relatives. He knew that, once he left, there was a chance he might never see them again. This thought saddened him, but the idea of becoming a missionary grew stronger every day.

When he was finally able to present himself at the office of the church missionary society, he was told to report to Highbury College for training as a medical missionary. He threw himself into his studies enthusiastically, knowing that the sooner he completed the courses, the sooner he could be on his way to some distant shore.

Once in a while his mind wandered. Where will it be? China? Africa? South America?

Fate made the decision when his two years of training were up. One afternoon a Naval officer appeared in the missionary offices and asked to talk to Dr. Alford, who was in charge.

He leaned forward earnestly as he spoke to the doctor. "My name is Captain Prevost. I have begged the Church of England to send a missionary to Port Simpson on the coast of British Columbia. They cannot see their way clear to do it. I now come to you."

He paused and frowned slightly. "I should tell you that whoever goes must have exceptional courage and determination. He will also need good sound business judgment, since he will have full responsibility for the entire mission. Most of all he must have unlimited faith in the Almighty."

"Picking the right man is not the only problem," said Dr. Alford. "Our society does not have the money to establish a new mission. Would you be willing to help us raise funds?"

"Not only that, but I'll give him free passage on board my ship. You just worry about finding the right man for the job." The captain rose, turned, and walked briskly out of the office.

There was no doubt in anyone's mind that William Duncan was the man for the new post. Dr. Alford called him into his office and told him of the dangers, of the responsibility, of the risks he would be taking if he accepted.

"Any missionary sent there will be taking his life in his hands," he said.

William replied instantly. "I told you I'll go wherever I'm sent."

Dr. Alford smiled. "Can you be ready by next Tuesday?"

"If necessary, I can be ready within an hour," said William.

His ship dropped anchor in a harbor near Victoria, British Columbia, on June 13, 1857. William was eager to begin his work. He had no idea that his first major obstacle would be an official of the Hudson's Bay Company. He had won his argument with him, but as he left the office, he realized that the dangers which awaited him might be greater than he had imagined. As happy as he was to be only 600 miles from his post, he knew that he was only one man. He would be alone among hundreds of savages. Would they let him live long enough to give them his message?■

2

What Can One Man Do?

Williiam found that even with the permission he had received, he would not be able to leave Victoria until September. There were only two steamers going north every year, and one of them had left a short while before he arrived. He was invited to stay at the home of the Reverend and Mrs. Edward Cridge. William helped the Reverend conduct church services and direct the choir. Before his visit was over, they had become good friends.

A British official, the Honorable W. J. MacDonald, often visited at the Cridges' home. William formed a lasting friendship also with him.

Both men tried to talk William into changing his mind about going north. "There is so much work to be done right here," they said. "Why must you endanger your life while trying to do something that is impossible?"

"You should have listened to the Hudson's Bay man," said Mr.

MacDonald. "He knows what the situation there is really like."

"I appreciate your concern," said William, "but I must go ahead and complete my mission."

William knew that he had to find a way to communicate with the natives. He studied Chinook, which is not a real language. It had been invented by the traders to be used to conduct business with the Indians.

One day he happened to meet a Tsimshian Indian. He was a friendly, intelligent man who offered to teach him the Tsimshian language. William studied eagerly every chance he got. He knew that being able to communicate with his flock might mean the difference between success and failure.

He was bitterly disappointed when his teacher had to leave after just a few lessons.

"Thank you," he said, grasping the Indian's hand. "I am grateful for your help."

"I am sorry I cannot stay longer," said the Indian. "I will tell my tribe that you are coming and ask them to treat you well."

After he left, William grew impatient having to wait for the steamer. He was more anxious than ever to start his work.

Finally September arrived, and with it the steamer. William said good-bye to his friends and gathered his baggage together. He was taking medical supplies and carpentering and blacksmithing tools. He wanted to be ready for whatever he was called upon to do.

The trip promised to be a delightful one. For five days William gazed upon sparkling blue inlets and fjords, the wide, smooth channels of the sea, with a sandy shore on one side and tree-covered islands on the other. As the steamer progressed northward, there were the mountain peaks of Vancouver Island and the distant snow-covered mountains on the mainland.

He delighted in watching the antics of a herd of whales as they spouted and dove and surfaced. Dozens of porpoises followed the steamer and seemed to be playing tag with each other.

So far the Northland had held no terrors for William. He felt uplifted and filled with the desire to spread the Gospel, and he knew that nothing would stand in his way.

Then one morning the steamer made its way into Discovery Passage and from there into Seymour Narrows. William stood on the deck with one of the crew members and watched the swirling, frothing currents beat against the sharp-edged reef in the center of the channel. The ship groaned and swayed as it slowly made its way through the rushing waters. A shudder went through its hulk, and William gripped the railing until his knuckles turned white.

"The natives call this passage 'Yaculta,'" said his companion gloomily. "That means 'The Home of the Evil Spirits.' There's been many a ship dashed against that reef. All of them sank 100 fathoms down."

Like a magnet the reef seemed to draw the ship towards it. William shut his eyes and prayed. He hadn't come this far to die before he preached the Gospel to the Indians.

When he looked again, the ship was veering away from the jagged rocks and was on its way out of the narrows. William's prayers had been answered.

A few hours later William saw crude huts lining the shore. Many had a totem pole in front of them.

A crew member approached him. "Those totems are really works of art. When you get a chance you should examine some of them. Starting from the time the Indian picks out a log and starts to carve it, it could take years before it's finished."

"But what do they mean?" asked William.

"Each one shows the family history of the natives who live in the hut. They tell about the legends and achievements of their ancestors. The figure on the top is the wife's tribal totem. She's considered the head of the family. Right under that is the husband's."

"A visiting native passing by can tell which clan the people in the hut belong to. If he sees that the wife belongs to the same clan he does, he feels free to stop in and stay as long as he wants. No native has to want for food and rest if he can find the right totem."

"Why, those poles mean about the same thing to an Indian that our coat-of-arms does to us back in England," said William.

"That's the idea," said his companion. "The natives are very proud of those totems."

"And well they should be," replied William. He was glad he'd had this talk. No man or woman who was as proud of their ancestry and family as these people were could be called savage or uncivilized. He was convinced that his friends had exaggerated the danger he was walking into.

This confident mood continued until the steamer approached the northern end of Vancouver Island. There were large birds flying in circles about the beach. William was standing alone at the rail and saw some dark objects strewn about. He squinted his eyes and tried to make out what they were. Were they dead animals? Had someone been hunting and left the carcasses to rot on the sand?

Then he drew back in revulsion. There were human limbs—an arm, a leg—there were at least five disemboweled bodies there in front of him. And those birds—he knew now that they were vultures. He swallowed hard and breathed deeply, fighting a rising tide of nausea. Dear God, this was what he had been hearing about. Savagery, cannibalism, men who behaved like animals. What could he do—one man who could not even speak their language?

William was only vaguely aware of the breathtaking scenery for the rest of the trip. Visions of the endless circling of the vultures over those pitiful remains of human beings stayed with him like a suffocating cloud. He spent hours on his knees praying for a renewal of his courage and strength of purpose. He knew he would never be useful as an instrument of God unless he could walk confident and serene among the natives. He was beginning to despair that he would ever be able to recapture that spirit which filled him when he left England.

Then, just before the steamer approached the end of his journey, his prayers were answered. He saw the snow-clad mountains, the waterfalls and green valleys, and the deer drinking from the clear springs which trickled down the hillsides. The beauty of the panorama filled his heart, and the cloud disappeared.

"Thank You, Lord," he prayed silently. "Forgive me for doubting. You sent me here to do a job, and with Your help I will do it." ■

3

Fear Thrives in the Hearts of Men

William's ship dropped anchor at Port Simpson at midnight on Oct. 1, 1857. For a few moments he stood looking at the night-shrouded shore. There was a fort, silent and dark, and the whole scene had a dreamlike quality to it. The only sign of life was the flickering of scattered bonfires. He could barely make out a few small huts, which were set up on stilts to raise them up out of the reach of the tides. They were clustered on each side of the fort.

Then the ship's whistle blew sharply, cutting into the still, cold air, and William knew this was no dream. Within 10 minutes there were lights and voices coming from inside the fort. The big gates swung open, and several men came down to the water line. William followed Captain Prevost into the small landing craft and shivered as the damp air clung to him. The sailors put their oars into the water. There was no turning back now.

Suddenly a shadowy figure climbed down from one of the huts. As it emerged from the shadows of the trees, William saw that

it was a naked man. The man lit a long torch from one of the bonfires and ran with great strides along the shore. One by one other men joined him until the beach was alive with them. They broke into a wild dance, prancing and jumping and shouting in their strange tongue. The light from their torches reflected upon their glistening bodies, and William saw that they were covered with yellowish streaks of paint.

He gazed with fascinated horror as the realization grew upon him that this was his congregation.

"Good evening, Captain Prevost." The man who appeared to be the leader of the men from the fort spoke as the landing vessel approached the shore.

"Good evening, sir," replied the captain as he stepped from the boat. "May I present William Duncan? He has come to minister to the Tsimshians. He is to stay at the fort under your protection."

The man seemed to be studying William as he extended his hand. "I am Captain Lewis," he said formally. "It is a pity we did not know you were arriving. We have no quarters prepared for you."

There was a tone of hostility in Captain Lewis' voice. In spite of the quick handshake, William felt that he was not entirely welcome at Port Simpson. "Perhaps I should spend the remainder of the night on the ship," he said. "I do not want to inconvenience anyone at this hour."

"That is a good idea," said the captain, turning abruptly. He headed toward the fort, followed by his heavily armed men.

Odd, thought William. But then perhaps I am overly tired and am imagining things. And after all, we awoke the captain from a sound sleep. He has a right to be touchy.

He turned back to the landing craft, then sensed that someone was staring at him. When he looked, he found himself staring directly into a pair of glittering, black eyes. There was a natural curiosity in the Indian's gaze, but there was more. A deep distrust, perhaps hate, lay somewhere inside his head.

A shiver ran through William as he took his place in the boat. He was overwhelmingly grateful for the security and protection the steamship offered.

Prayer and a few hours of sleep refreshed William. By dawn he felt he could respond to the challenges he had felt earlier. As he stepped onto the muddy shore, the ferocious-looking naked men who had been running on the beach were standing in sullen groups in front of the huts. Women and children sat huddled under dirty, ragged blankets and stared dully at the armed soldiers who escorted William into the fort.

Even before he entered the metal-sheathed double gates of the fort, he had decided to talk to Captain Lewis about providing some warm jackets and shirts for the natives. He didn't see how he could preach about the warmth of God's love when they were shivering in the winds of winter.

Both doors were bolted and barred behind him as soon as he was inside. William glanced up and saw an armed sentry pacing steadily back and forth upon a gallery ramp which had been erected around the entire inside of the fort 4 feet below the top of the outer wall.

He frowned. "You seem to live in fear," he said to a soldier standing nearby. "Are these precautions necessary all the time?"

"I certainly wouldn't step outside of these walls without a rifle and a few of my friends to accompany me," replied the soldier. "Maybe you didn't notice the bullet holes and the arrows that scar the outer wall. You just can't trust those savages. When they go on the warpath, nothing stands in their way. And you never know what will set them off."

"Do you mean to say that you live in fear behind these walls all year round?"

"Most of the time," replied the soldier. "We have no need to go out very often. The men have their wives here and we have our own blacksmith shop and everything we need to live. When we do go out to cut wood or to hunt, we carry guns and shoot the Indians at the first suspicious move. After all, there are hundreds of them and only 25 of us. We have to be cautious or we'll pay with our lives."

William glanced up at the sentinal again. Then for the first time he noticed the four cannons, one at each corner of the stockade.

Fear thrives in the hearts of these men, he thought. I saw it also in the eyes of that Indian last night. I cannot believe that God meant for His children to live like this—shut off from each other in hatred and distrust.

William spent the day meeting the people who lived within the fortress walls and asking questions of them. Soldiers and men of the Hudson's Bay Company shared the work and the living quarters. There was a medium-sized building which housed the captain and which also contained the mess hall. The second officer was quartered in a smaller building. It was here that William was given two rooms. The rest of the men and their wives lived in a single large building which contained five rooms.

There was also a company store and a huge warehouse. William gasped when he saw the thousands of valuable furs that were stacked in the warehouse. Mink, wolverine, sable, and sea otter pelts were piled to the ceiling. He couldn't begin to calculate the wealth which lay in front of him.

Why, then, were the natives just outside of these walls shivering in ragged blankets? Hadn't they caught the animals from which these pelts came? Shouldn't they be prospering as a result of their efforts?

William decided to ask Captain Lewis the answers to those questions.

The following day as he was looking for the captain, William passed by the warehouse. The guard at the gate was letting two Indians at a time into the fort. They carried their armloads of glossy, thick pelts to the warehouse, while watchful men armed with rifles followed closely behind them.

William stood to one side as they bartered with the clerk. For four marten pelts one Indian received only a piece of soap as big as a finger. A beautiful sea otter skin was traded for about three dollars worth of goods at the company store.

William was aghast. Why, the Indians were being cheated

outrageously, he thought. Is it possible that Captain Lewis has given permission for such thievery?

As the other Indians waiting outside the gate were let in, the same sort of uneven bargaining occurred. The little money they received was just enough to keep them in food and other supplies they bought from the company store. William no longer had to talk to Captain Lewis about why the Indians were so poor. The answer was right there in front of him.

The last pair of Indians finished their business, and William followed them to the gate. There was something about one of them that caught his eye. He stood straight and tall, and there was an unusually intelligent light in his expression.

William turned to a young workman. "Do you know the name of that Indian who just left—the tall one?"

The workman nodded. "Yes, that was Clah. He comes here often. The captain has no love for him."

William resolved to find out more about Clah. He had a feeling that this proud Indian could do much for him. But first he had to talk to Captain Lewis. He knew it would do no good for him to preach God's love to the natives unless the white men could show them by their example what that love meant.

For the next three weeks William tried to talk to the captain about getting clothing for the Indians and treating them more fairly. The officer's attitude remained cool, and for the last few days he had actually seemed to be avoiding William. He was definitely unreceptive to any suggestions William had about improving the treatment of the Tsimshians.

On Sunday William readied the mess hall for the service he conducted for the men of the fort. As he placed the chairs and collected the notes for his sermon, his mind was troubled. He knew that he could not give up on his fight to obtain fair treatment for the natives. There must be some way to convince the captain of the benefit such treatment would bring to everyone. William was going to have to find that way.

He glanced around the room. Satisfied with how it looked, he quickly ate his breakfast, which was by now quite cold. When he had finished, he went to the door to await the men and their wives. He was pleased at how eagerly they listened to his sermons and how quickly they were learning to read and write in their spare time. They had all come from poor families and were happy for the chance to receive an education. To be able to read God's Word as well as to hear it was something most of them had thought they would never be able to do.

William's eyes narrowed when he saw five men with work clothes walk toward the gate. They all had axes over their shoulders. Didn't they realize it was the Sabbath and that it was time for the service to begin?

He quickly located the second officer. "I just saw some men leaving the fort to chop wood. Why are they doing that?"

"Why, the captain told them to," the officer replied.

Anger welled up within William, and he did not trust himself to approach Captain Lewis. He scratched out a message.

"Sir," he wrote, "I cannot hold any services in the fort today. I am no hypocrite. You and I both know that you have just broken one of God's commandments."

"Please see that the captain gets this immediately," he told the officer. Then he strode off to his quarters to wait for the answer.

Ten minutes later there was a loud banging on his door. When William opened it, Captain Lewis stood there. His face was red and his fists were clenched.

"I have received your letter, sir," he said. "I thought when you came you would try to run this fort, and I see that I was right."

William kept a tight rein on his anger. "Not at all, sir. I try to run nothing. I issue no orders, only to myself. I don't prevent your having a service. I simply say that I will have no part in it, knowing that God's law as to the Sabbath is being openly broken."

"Well, sir, I shall report this assumption of authority to the Hudson's Bay Company."

"All right, do so. I will also make my report, and I have no fear of the result," replied William calmly.

The captain stared at him for a moment, then turned on his heel and marched away. Soon William heard his angry voice. "Go after those men and tell them to stop their work. It seems that someone else is going to run things in the fort after this."

William bowed his head and prayed. "Please forgive me for my anger, Father. I cannot stand by and see Your Commandments shattered."

As he walked back to the mess hall, he felt that the incident was a troubling indication of the future. Ministering to the Indians was going to be a tremendous task, but he knew that with God's help he could do it.

But what about those among his own people who chose to oppose him? And what about his own stubborn anger? Would he be able to overcome these additional obstacles?■

4

Clah Teaches William

William knew that he could not let any doubts or problems stand in the way of his mission. He decided to deal with Captain Lewis day by day, and he hoped to overcome his own character flaws by prayer and effort. He would have to learn to give in when necessary and to stand up for what he knew to be right when the occasion called for it.

Right now his immediate need was to learn the Tsimshian language. Chinook was all right as a temporary means of communication, but in order to express what was deep in his heart, he had to be able to speak freely and easily with the natives. He waited for Clah to come into the fort again. William had decided that the stately Indian would be the ideal person to be his teacher.

Two weeks later Clah came to do some trading. William waited until he was through with his business, then approached him. By combining sign language and Chinook, William managed to say that he wanted to learn to speak in the Tsimshian tongue.

Clah frowned. He didn't seem to understand. William haltingly repeated the request. The Indian shook his head slowly, as if he was bewildered.

William thought quickly. He didn't know how else to state his request. He repeated it slowly and as clearly as he could.

Clah interrupted him before he was finished. "I understand your question," he said in Chinook. "What amazes me is why you should want to learn my language. No other white man has ever wanted to do that."

"Not only that," replied William. "I also want to learn as much as possible about your way of life. Will you help me? I would appreciate it deeply."

Clah shrugged. "Certainly I will help. You must have your reasons."

William clasped the Indian's hands. "Good. Let us start tomorrow. I am eager to begin."

During the next few weeks William and Clah worked together every day. Clah was a tireless teacher, but he was also a good pupil. He was learning English as fast as William was learning Tsimshian. They spent hours pointing out various objects and exchanging the Indian and English words for them. Then William wrote out a list of 1,500 common words. After explaining their meaning to Clah, the Indian told him the Tsimshian equivalents for them.

. During the time they spent together William learned that the Indians eked out a bare existence by trapping furs and fishing. Every summer most of the men left the village to go up the Nass River to fish for oolakan, or candlefish. These fish were so oily that they could be dried and supplied with a wick and used as candles. The Indians used the oil for cooking and eating. They also ate halibut and wild berries which grew along the banks of the rivers.

Clah said that there were 2,300 Tsimshians living near Port Simpson and they were divided into nine tribes, each living in its own village. Each tribe, however, contained members of the same four clans, so all of the villages were bound together by close family ties.

"Is it true that your people eat the flesh of humans?" William asked one day. He had never been able to erase the memory of the torn limbs he had seen on the beach.

Clah hesitated, then answered slowly. "Yes, some of them do, but the cannibals are all members of only one tribe. They eat human flesh during many of their ceremonies. If they do not have a dead body to use, they go out and kill the first stranger they see."

William swallowed hard. So the stories of cannibalism were true, but evidently Clah was not proud of that fact. He and the Indian sat quietly for a few moments until William decided to change the subject. The Indian seemed ill at ease after talking of such atrocities.

"I saw some of your tribesmen bring their canoes in from a storm yesterday," he said. "They put the most practiced mariners with the best equipment to shame."

Clah raised his head and smiled. His eyes were glowing with pride at William's praise of his people.

William and Clah had been studying each other's language for several weeks when a young chief came to William's door one afternoon. He said he was a close friend of Clah's and wanted to speak to William. William invited him into his small front room and asked him to sit down, but the Indian continued to stand, shifting uneasily from one foot to another.

"What is it?" William asked gently.

"Clah has been telling the members of my tribe about you," replied the Indian. "We do not understand a white man who does not come among us to sell whiskey or trade furs."

Small pricks of excitement touched William's body. The Indians were already curious about him—were asking questions. This was a good sign.

"It is true. I come among you to do neither. I wish your people well and would like to help them better their lives—to tell them of their Father's love."

"No other white man has ever wanted such things for the Indians."

"God wants those things for you. I am here only to give you that message."

The Indian looked around the room. "I have heard that you have come here with the letter of God. Is that so? Have you the letter of God with you?"

"I have." William's voice was calm, but his heart was pounding with anticipation.

"Would you mind showing it to me?"

William went into the other room and returned with his large, well-worn Bible. He placed it on the table. "This is God's book."

The Indian reverently laid his hand upon it. "Then is God's letter for the Tsimshians also? Does this book give God's heart to us?"

"Certainly. God sent this book to your people as well as to mine."

"And are you going to tell the Indians that?"

"I am," replied William softly.

"Ahm! Ahm! It is good! It is good!" said the Indian. "I will leave now."

William watched him as he walked toward the gate with the armed soldiers watching him alertly. Soon they will put those rifles down, he thought. White men and Indians will live side by side in peace and love. He knelt to pray. His heart was so overflowing with joy that he could not hold it all inside of him.

"You are insane to think you can go out among those savages unarmed!" shouted Captain Lewis the next day. "You are housed in this fort, and that makes you my responsibility. If you want to preach to them, you can do it within the walls of the stockade while

34

my men have their rifles trained upon them."

William had not thought that telling the captain of his plans to go among the Indians would bring on this tirade. The more the soldier shouted, the more stubborn William grew. "It cannot be done in that manner," he said. "Men cannot learn about the Prince of peace while they have guns pointed at their heads. No, with or without your permission, I must go among them in my own way and at my own time."

"Don't you understand? You may well be killed! You've never heard their unearthly screams and the beating of their drums as they conduct their heathen ceremonies using their human sacrifices. I have seen them with human heads, still dripping blood, hanging from their belts."

William shook his head quickly to wipe the picture from his mind. "That may well be true. All the more reason why I must go out among them."

The next day William was standing on the gallery ramp talking to the sentinal. The weather was crisp and cold, signaling the nearness of winter. A movement outside the gate caught his eye. An Indian, laden down with furs, was waiting to be admitted to the fort. A soldier started to unbolt the inner gate.

At that moment William saw a native come from behind a clump of trees at the side of the fort. Quickly the native raised a rifle to his shoulder, aimed, and fired. The Indian at the gate fell, blood spurting from a wound in his side.

William ran down the stairs to the ground. "Hurry!" he shouted. "A man is bleeding to death out there."

The guard finished bolting the gate securely, then turned and looked at William.

"Quickly!" William was desperate now. "The man needs help immediately!"

"It's a problem for the Indians to settle," said the guard.

William was stunned. He started to unbar the gate himself,

calling for someone to get his medical kit. Suddenly strong arms grabbed him. "Don't be a fool," said a workman. "You'll be killed if you go out there."

William turned and twisted angrily. When he had freed himself, he found that the guard was standing in front of the gate with his rifle in his hands.

William raced to a peephole and looked out. The man was still lying on the ground, writhing and groaning. Then before his horrified gaze, two natives appeared accompanied by the man who had fired the shot.

"Finish what I started," said the assailant in a commanding voice.

The two men each fired at the helpless victim. When he had stopped moving, they pulled his body after them and disappeared into the woods.

William felt the blood leaving his face. Weakly he turned and faced the guard.

"That was Legaic, one of the Tsimshian chiefs," said the guard. "He's a murderous devil—can't be trusted."

Legaic—Clah had mentioned the name several times. He was a powerful chief. Can even God's love soften that hard, brutal heart? William wondered. And do I have the courage to face such a man?

As William stumbled away, he realized that the worst side of what he had just seen was that the members of his own race had ignored a man's cry for help. They seemed to care nothing for the fact that a murder had been committed just a few feet away from them.

If my so-called civilized people are so hardened, how am I ever going to convince the Indians that they should turn away from such a way of life?

I must pray, he decided. I must ask for wisdom and understanding and serenity and I must go out among them. He knew that every day spent in hesitation and indecision might mean another meaningless death.■

5

William Begins His Work

"We will have no lesson today, Clah," said William the following morning. "I want to go out among your people and become acquainted with them. I will take my medical bag in case there are any sick that I can help."

Clah nodded. "This is good. My people have been asking when they can see and talk to you."

"Do you think I speak your language well enough to talk to them?"

"You have learned well and quickly. I have no difficulty understanding you when you speak in my tongue," replied Clah.

"All right. We shall go now." William picked up his medical bag and walked toward the gate with Clah behind him.

The guard opened the gate to let the Indian out, but stood in front of William barring his way. "Do you have permission to leave, sir?" he asked.

"I need no permission. I am going out to meet my congregation."

The guard glanced over William's shoulder and an expression of relief spread over his face. William turned and faced Captain Lewis.

"Where do you think you're going?" the captain blustered. "If you want to leave, I will send a few riflemen along to protect you. Don't you recall what happened just outside these walls yesterday? And that was one of their own."

"I saw, and that is why I must go out and speak to the natives," said William resolutely. He wished he could push the memory of blood and gunshots and glittering black eyes filled with hate from his mind.

The captain's face turned a deeper shade of red. "You insist on having your own way—defying my authority. Well, go ahead, it's your neck. I wash my hands of you."

"Thank you, Captain. I assure you that I will walk in safety. You need feel no responsibility for my actions. My life is in the hands of the Lord."

William turned. The guard glanced at Captain Lewis, then unbarred and unbolted the gates. William took a deep breath and bowed his head. "Lord, it is in Your hands. Please allow me to give these men and women Your sacred message."

Then he looked at Clah and smiled. "Let us go. We have much to do today."

William went from village to village, spending an equal amount of time in each one. He saw small naked children running and playing games of tag. Their arms and legs were thin, but their eyes flashed with excitement and glee. There were older children huddled in groups, staring at William with questioning expressions. There were women cooking meager meals of fish and potatoes, and men sharpening their spears on rocks and mending their fishing nets.

He entered huts in which sick children and old men and women lay under ragged blankets on dirt floors.

One small boy was hot with fever, and his breath came out in gasping wheezes. His mother hovered anxiously nearby as William reached into his bag and pulled out a vial of liquid. As he put a spoonful of the medicine into the boy's mouth, the woman clasped her hands together and frowned.

William smoothed the hair back from the boy's flushed face and spoke reassuringly to him. Then he turned to the mother. "He will be fine," he said. "I will return tomorrow to check on him."

As William continued on his visits to the various tribes, most of the natives seemed more interested in touching his sleeve and playing with the buttons on his coat than in listening to what he had to say to them. William didn't mind. He knew they would listen carefully when they were ready.

As he and Clah walked back to the fort at the end of the day, William offered a silent prayer of thanks. There had been no problems, no threats—nothing but a constant questioning in the eyes of the natives. He knew that with God's help he would be able to show them how good their lives could be. He also knew that it would take more than prayer.

He turned to Clah. "Your people will never be free from illness until they sleep under clean blankets and have clean houses. Disease lurks in dirt."

"That will not be easy," said Clah. "You have seen how many skins we must give to get a small sliver of soap. Soap costs too much for us to use it freely."

William resolved to do something about the soap supply. The next day when he returned to the villages he brought several cakes of laundry soap that he had brought with him from England for his own use. The Indians looked at it wonderingly, running their hands over it and murmuring to each other. Then they smiled and nodded their heads.

"They say it is good," said Clah. "They have never received such gifts from a white man."

William looked in on the sick boy he had treated the day before. His mother greeted him with a smile and pointed to the child. "See, he is almost ready to run and play once more," she said. The boy looked at William wide-eyed.

"Indeed, he does look much better," said William. "No more medicine for him."

William left the hut and walked to the edge of the village to join Clah. As he walked he realized that someone was watching his every move. He turned and looked at an older man who had been following him. With a start William realized that the man was the one who had shot down the Indian at the gate.

Legaic! William had heard that name many times since the day he had first seen him. He was a powerful chieftain, known for his quick temper and brutality. Even now, William could see that the other Indians drew back from him and left him alone.

Clah appeared from one of the huts, and a feeling of relief washed over William. Now he could leave this place and go back to the safety of the fortress walls. He started to walk briskly toward Clah, half expecting to feel an arrow in his back at any moment.

What am I doing? he thought. If I run away from Legaic now, I will find it twice as hard to face him next time. He straightened his shoulders, turned around, and headed straight toward the grim-faced chief.

"I have brought soap to your people today," said William. "Soon I would like to bring a message from the heavenly Father."

Legaic stared coldly at him and did not answer. Then he grunted and walked away in the opposite direction.

William walked thoughtfully back to Clah. "I wish I knew what was going on deep in that man's mind," he said. "If I could find the key to his heart, I might win the entire tribe over to the side of God."

"Do not hope for too much at first," said Clah. "Legaic's heart is perhaps the hardest of all."

Legaic hovered in the background like a dark shadow every

41

time William went into his village. He never spoke—just watched and waited.

Waiting for what? wondered William with a shiver. He had to ignore the chief and carry on his business as if he weren't there. If he dwelled on the dark looks the Indian sent his way, he would never have the courage to walk among the people of his tribe.

The furtive, distrusting looks of the other Indians were slowly changing into shy smiles and hands extended in greeting. Their acceptance of William's visits was growing, and he wasn't going to let one dour-faced chief stop him.

I wish I felt as welcome with Captain Lewis as I do with most of the Indians, he thought one day as he read a message he had just received. It said that the captain wanted to see him as soon as possible. William knew that every time he got a message like that, it meant trouble. He sighed. He had been looking forward to a quick supper, some Bible study, and an early bedtime. Instead he trudged wearily to the captain's quarters.

"Come in," a gruff voice said when William knocked on the door.

"You wanted to see me, Captain Lewis?"

"I certainly do." The captain's face was grim. "Just what do you think your duties are here anyway?"

"Wh-why to minister to my congregation." William was bewildered.

"Do you think they include providing the natives with supplies to the detriment of the trading post? You are aware, are you not, that the Hudson's Bay Company has trade agreements with the tribes, and that these agreements were drawn up for the mutual benefit of everyone?"

William remained silent. He did not agree that the agreements were mutually beneficial. It seemed to him that the Indians usually came out on the short end of the stick.

"We of course expect you not to interfere in those trade agreements," said the captain.

"Please get to the point, sir," said William. "I am completely at a loss as to your meaning, and I am very tired."

"What I mean is that you have been giving soap away to the Indians. We cannot have you giving away what we have always used as a trading tool."

All this just because of a few bars of soap! Anger boiled up within William and some of it had to spill out. "That little sliver of soap!" he shouted. "That little sliver of soap which you exchange for a fortune in pelts! Yes, I have seen your clerks in action. The Indians are being woefully cheated, and if it is within my power, I intend to correct that situation."

The captain rose from his chair. "You are <u>not</u> to give the natives any more soap. Is that understood? You are directly interfering with the smooth running of this fort when you disregard my instructions. I will have you removed from the area if you continue."

William bowed his head slightly. "I understand, sir. I will give the Indians no more soap." Trembling with anger, he backed out of the room.

By the time he reached his quarters, the anger had dissolved, and a slight smile played around his lips. I will keep my promise. I will no longer give the Indians soap. I shall teach them how to make their own.■

6

The Stone Wall Begins to Crumble

The Indian women learned quickly, and soon every tribe had a constant supply of soap. Cooking utensils were now cleaned after each use, and the bare wooden floors of the huts in the woods were scrubbed until they began losing their accumulation of grease and dirt. The word began to spread about the marvelous medicines that William carried in his black bag. Natives told each other about the woman who had had the terrible pains in her stomach, but who had been magically cured when William gave her some pills. They expressed amazement at the children who were up running and playing when just hours earlier they had been feverish and crying.

William and Clah were walking along the shore one Saturday morning. "To think that just a few weeks ago I was in fear of my life. I can't tell you how I trembled the first time I went among your people."

Clah nodded. "It is true. You have made great headway. But your troubles are not yet over. The medicine men and many of the chiefs are still your enemies. They do not like to see the power you are gaining over their people. They are the ones you will have to win over before your position is secure."

William did not reply. He knew that Clah was right. Just yesterday he had seen a great crowd of natives taking to their canoes and paddling quickly away from shore. When he had asked Clah what was happening, the Indian had answered solemnly, "The medicine men are looking for a human body to use in a ceremony. If they do not find one who is already dead, they will kill someone. Those people are taking to the sea to save their lives."

William knew that he was going to have to spread God's Word more quickly. He had wanted to take more time to get to know the natives before he had any sort of formal service. Now he knew he could not wait.

"Clah," he said, "I am going to write a message to the chief of each tribe, and I would like you to deliver them for me this afternoon. Tomorrow I would like to preach my first sermon to them."

Clah came to William's quarters that afternoon. His eyes were burning with excitement. "They all said yes! They all said yes! They would like to hear what you have to say. Oh, sir, this is indeed a wonderful thing."

William reached for Clah's hands and pressed them between his own. "My friend, I owe so much to you. It is only because of the hours that you have spent helping me learn your language that I shall be able to deliver this sermon. I want you to sit beside me tomorrow as I speak. I want them to know that you are my friend."

When Clah had gone, William went to the calendar on his wall and drew a big circle around the next day's date—June 13, 1858. Such an important day, he thought. Oh, how I pray that the natives will be moved to accept my message and that the hearts of the

45

chieftains and the medicine men will be softened. A vision of Legaic's face flashed through his mind. If I could only make him understand God's love, I would feel as if I had torn down a stone wall.

The first tribe was gathered in their meeting hall by the time William arrived. He looked out upon their faces, some stony and defiant, some expectant, some eager, and his confidence wavered. He had been up almost all night picking just the right words to say, but now words suddenly seemed so weak against the age-old heathenish habits of these people. What if he couldn't make them understand? What if he angered them by using the wrong words? The mispronunciation of one word could lead to a wrong interpretation and a complete misunderstanding of what he was trying to say.

He leaned toward Clah and whispered, "Perhaps I should read the sermon to you sentence by sentence and have you interpret the words for the congregation."

Clah shook his head emphatically. "That would only make things worse. I have told my people that you have gone to all the trouble of learning their language. This has impressed them deeply, for no other white man ever did this. For you to deliver the message now in English would brand me as a liar and you as a man who is not what he professes to be. Other white men have talked to them about God, but have failed in their mission because the Indians didn't trust them. Don't disappoint them now."

William felt suddenly humble. This uneducated native was so much wiser than he in so many ways. "You are right, my friend," he murmured. "I was being foolish."

He turned to shut the door behind him and stood facing it for several seconds, praying silently for guidance. All the while he felt the eyes of his congregation upon him.

Suddenly filled with strength, he turned to face the natives and fell to his knees. He prayed aloud in the Tsimshian language, and

46

the words flowed easily from his tongue. He felt as though he had been speaking their language all his life.

Then he rose to his feet and launched right into his sermon. His message was short, simple, and direct. He spoke of the Bible and of the way God saw every man as he went about his daily life.

"Jesus Christ suffered and died for our sins," he concluded. "He is now in heaven to hear and answer our prayers. He bids us to put away our sinful ways and look to Him to be saved. If we obey, He will pardon our sins, make us holy, and take us to live with Him in heaven when we die. I exhort you not to reject God's message of love. Put away your evil ways and learn God's ways. Believe that God is longing to bless you and to save you."

When the final words had been spoken, he asked the Indians to kneel with him and to pray. To a man, they joined with him on their knees as William poured forth words of thanks.

They went from village to village until they came to the last, the village of Legaic and his tribe. When he entered the meeting house, William was dismayed to see several soldiers from the fort among the 150 people in the room.

Why did Captain Lewis order these men to be here? William wondered angrily. I don't want Legaic or anyone to think that I have to aim a gun at his head to make him listen to me.

Clah seemed to know what he was thinking. "I believe the soldiers are here because Legaic has such a bad reputation."

William saw the chief sitting toward the back of the room. His arms were folded across his chest, and he seemed to be daring William to start his sermon.

"I heard that Legaic has told his people to sit quietly and to listen to what you have to say. You have caught his attention, although he does not like to show that he has any interest in what you say."

"If only that is so," said William. He took a deep breath,

ignored the rifles of the soldiers, ignored Legaic's icy stare, and launched into his opening prayer.

The sermon was over, the Indians were filing out of the door, and William stood by himself in a corner of the room. He felt weak and tired and was anxious to return to the fort and shut himself away in his rooms. *Maybe I should have waited—I am trying too hard and the Indians can sense how ill at ease I am.*

All the reasons why he shouldn't have attempted to give a full-fledged sermon this soon went through his tired mind. With his shoulders slumped he walked to the door, looking for Clah.

He spotted him talking to another Indian several yards away. He talked a few more moments, then waved and headed in William's direction. A wide grin lit up his face.

"Legaic wishes you to start a school in his village. He has heard how you have taught the white soldiers to read and write, and he wishes you to do the same for the people of his tribe."

William felt himself staring in disbelief. "This is beyond my wildest dreams," he said. "Legaic of all men! And just a few minutes ago I was thinking that I had failed completely. My prayers have been so quickly answered."

He turned his face upward. "O Lord, forgive me for doubting the power of Your Word."

William didn't waste any time. The following Wednesday he held his first classes—the children in the morning and the adults in the afternoon. They met in the meetinghouse of Legaic's tribe, but Clah let everyone know that anyone from any of the tribes could attend. There were 26 children present at the first roll call. By the following month the small building could barely hold all the eager pupils.

"What we need," William said to Clah one day, "is a big central

48

building which would be large enough for everyone who wishes to attend school."

"I agree," replied Clah. "It is the only way you will be able to reach everyone with equal force. It will build a unity among the tribes which will give them strength."

They went right to work picking out a good site for the new building, and by midsummer a spot on top of a hill which overlooked the bay had been cleared. Many of the men of the village had gone north for the fishing season, but everyone else— the older men, the women, and the children were spending all the time they could hauling brush away and cutting down trees and dragging logs up the hill. William staked out the dimensions of the building, and soon the foundation was in place. Every day William felt that working together was bringing them all closer than any words could have done.

One afternoon he was showing some boys how to apply pitch between the logs to make the building waterproof. A group of men were carrying a log up the hill, and William started down to help them up the last few feet.

Suddenly one of the men fell to the ground, clutching his chest and writhing in agony. William ran to his side and saw that his breath was coming out in painful gasps.

Heart attack, William thought quickly. He massaged the heaving chest and prayed to the Lord to release the man from his pain. He worked feverishly over the figure on the ground for over 30 minutes. Then, tired and defeated, he slumped over and said a final farewell to the still form.

He looked up, for the first time aware of the Indians staring down at him. "It was the Lord's will," he said. "This man was called to his heavenly home."

Why were they looking at him like that? Their faces were hard and cold. One by one they turned away and walked back down the hill. Finally William was left alone with the body and the hot sun beating down on his back.

Then like a flash William knew what was wrong. The natives had taken the man's death as an omen, a warning to stop their work on the building. Do they blame me? he wondered desperately. Have I lost everything because of a quirk of fate?

"Lord, o Lord, why did you take this man right at this time? Is all my work to be undone in this one stroke?"

Just one hour ago he had felt so confident, so sure of himself. Now what of his school? What of his entire mission? ■

7

William Challenges Legaic

A week went by, during which William prayed and pondered, and the construction of the schoolhouse came to a complete halt.

How the medicine men must be rejoicing, thought William. Anything that keeps the natives from becoming educated means that they will be ruled by superstition and false gods that much longer. Until the people learn to read and write and to trust in God's Word, they will be witnessing cannibalistic ceremonies and heathen mumbo jumbo.

William knew that he somehow had to convince the Indians that the workman's death was not a sign from the spirits warning them away from Christianity. And he had to do it soon. Precious days were slipping by.

The next day William and Clah went from village to village, trying to talk the natives into finishing the building.

"We cannot finish it," many of them replied. "Evil spirits hover over it."

Of course, thought William, that was the answer. He would abandon the original site and build another schoolhouse close to the bottom of the hill. The view would not be as beautiful, but they would be closer to the thick stand of trees. The workers would not have to spend long hours hauling logs up the hill.

William presented his idea to the Indians, then held his breath as they talked it over. There were low murmurs of conversation, then slowly the cautious nodding of heads.

"We will start on the new location tomorrow," was the answer from the leaders. "Perhaps the evil spirits will leave us alone there."

William did not correct them. It was enough that they had agreed to the construction of the new schoolhouse. They would learn soon enough that their evil spirits would disappear in the light of God's love.

The building was finished quickly and with no further problems. William stood on the hill overlooking it the night before the first classes were to be held in it. The scene was peaceful in the dusky light of evening, and although the chilly wind whipped his hair, William felt warm. He was thinking of all the willing hands who had helped complete the schoolhouse and of how he was standing alone and unafraid. It was hard to believe that just a year ago he had arrived at Port Simpson, and now here he was walking among the Indians as if he'd lived there all his life.

The beating of drums came from somewhere deep within the clump of trees by the school. His curiosity aroused, William followed the sound. After slipping quietly through the woods, he approached a clearing. There he stood in the shadows, frozen in horror. The body of a woman lay on the ground, and William watched through transfixed eyes as hideously painted men danced and chanted to the throbbing beat of the drums. A man in chieftain's robes hacked at the body with a knife and distributed bits of flesh to the dancers, who tore at it with their teeth.

William forced himself to tear his eyes away from the orgy and ran stumbling and sickened back to the safety of the fort.

Without saying a word to anyone, he went straight to his quarters, threw himself down on the bed, and tried to pray. For the first time in his life his prayers brought no peace.

Was it possible that Captain Lewis was right? Were the beliefs and habits of generations so deeply imbedded in the natives that even the love of God couldn't penetrate their hearts?

He woke early the next morning and gathered his books and other school supplies together. Last night's nightmarish scene was still clear in his mind, but he tried to concentrate on the work he had ahead of him. By the time he left his quarters the familiar stubbornness had stiffened his determination.

"Mr. Duncan, I would like to speak to you," called Captain Lewis as William walked by his office.

William walked into the small room and looked at the captain inquiringly.

"I must tell you that I have a message here from Legaic. He wants you to suspend the operation of your school and church for one month. The new building stands close to the spot where they conduct many of their rituals, and he says that the passing of the schoolchildren close by will interfere with the 'spirits' at work there." He paused and looked down at his desk. "I know we have not seen eye to eye on many subjects, but I truly feel a responsibility for you. I also have a great respect for you and the work you are attempting." He looked up again. "Last winter while they were practicing their heathenish rites you were spending most of your time behind the walls of the fort. Now you are constantly exposing yourself to the dangers which lie out there. I would advise you to heed Legaic's request. It won't hurt to lie low for a while."

William's mind raced. He was astounded at the fact that Legaic had requested the postponement of school instead of ordering it. After all, he didn't have to even allow William in his village if he didn't choose to.

On the other hand, it had been Legaic himself who had wanted William to start a regular school. Now that they had a new building and plenty of room for all the children who wanted to learn, the chief was asking William to make those children wait for the sake of the devil's work. And if he gave in to one chief, wouldn't any of the chiefs and the medicine men feel free to interfere with the school whenever they felt like it?

"I'm glad you are thinking it over," said Captain Lewis. "I hope you are coming to the right conclusion."

"I appreciate your concern, but I simply cannot allow anything or anyone to prevent the children from going to school. A month away from their studies would cause them great harm. I must keep the school open for the sake of everyone who wants to learn, and the church open for all those who want to receive God's message. I cannot allow the devil to rule in God's house."

Captain Lewis' breath came out slowly. "I have tried to warn you. Now your life is in your own hands."

"No, it is in God's hands," replied William. "I may not know what I am doing. If blood will be shed, it certainly will not be yours anyway. One thing I know, whether my blood will be shed or not, I could never afford to make a compromise with the devil."

William forced all thoughts of Legaic out of his head as he entered the schoolroom. It was early, and none of the pupils had arrived. As he laid his books on the desk, a voice called to him from the doorway. He turned quickly, ready for trouble.

The voice belonged to Legaic's wife. She was panting, and her face was troubled. "All the chiefs are gathered at my house and are prepared to start an important ceremony. Couldn't you please suspend school for just one day? It would save so much trouble for you."

William smiled at her. "Thank you for your concern, but I cannot. The children have much to learn, and to interrupt school constantly would discourage them."

"Could you stop for just one hour? I fear for your life."

"Even one hour away from the routine confuses the children. Every hour is important."

"The bell disturbs the ceremony," the woman said. "Could you not ring the bell today?"

"I'm sorry," replied William, "but I cannot do that either. If I didn't ring the bell, the children would think that there is no school and would not come."

The woman reached timidly for his arm. "I will pray for your life," she said softly, then scurried away.

As William watched her leave, he wavered in his resolution. After all, she wasn't asking for much—just one hour. Then he pressed his lips together and shook his head. No, he couldn't leave any room for the devil's work. If he allowed them one hour now, next time they would want an entire week. What then would the children think of Christians? That they preached God's love and yet turned their backs on the evil practices of the medicine men?

He turned and rang the school bell loudly and long.

Thirty minutes later William called the roll and found that only 80 out of the usual 150 students had answered the bell's call. Among those missing were some of his best scholars. He knew that their absence wasn't their fault. Their parents had kept them home because they were afraid of Legaic.

Whatever happens, thought William, I will not let any harm come to these innocent children. They must not pay for their elders' mistakes.

All morning he conducted the class in the usual manner, although he couldn't help walking to the door and looking out every few minutes. Then right after the lunch recess, he saw what he had been dreading. Several Indians were approaching the school. They walked single file, and Legaic himself was at the head of the line. William's stomach contracted when he saw the grotesque patterns of war paint on their bodies, and the masks covering their heads.

"Quickly, children, leave the room and hide under the building!" he shouted to his pupils. The children stood up without a question, and within seconds they were out the door and huddled together beneath the school.

William stood alone in the room, took a deep breath, folded his arms across his chest, and waited.

Legaic entered the room first, then seven other Indians followed and clustered around him.

"Why did you not obey my instructions?" Legaic growled. "I am chief here. You are nothing but an intruder in my land."

"This is God's land." William's heart was pounding, but his voice was calm. "He has granted all of us only the use of it. I am just representing Him and trying to tell you and your people of His love for you. Since He is my Master, and not you, it is His orders I must obey."

"You are a bad man!" Legaic stepped toward him, and William smelled liquor on his breath. "I have killed men before. I have made up my mind to punish you!" He pulled a knife and waved it in the air.

Another Indian, whom William knew by the name of Cushwaht, stepped up by Legaic's side. His eyes were fiery with rage. "Kill him! Kill him!" he cried. "Cut his head off! Give it to me and I will kick it on the beach!"

It's a nightmare, thought William desperately, but it's really happening. Has God chosen for me to die in this manner? He braced his legs, preparing to run for the door if there was an opening between the Indians. There was none. Instead, all of them closed in on him.

God, accept me if it is my time, William prayed quickly, but if it is Your wish, let me live and preach Your message here on earth.

"You would kill me, who have done you no harm." As William spoke, a calm settled over him. "I who have come here only for your good." He looked steadily at Legaic. Was that indecision he saw in his eyes? William's heart leaped when the chief stepped back and started lowering the knife.

Then Legaic glanced at Cushwaht, who was still chanting, "Kill him! Kill him!" in a monotone. The chief's face hardened and he raised the knife, pointed the tip at William's chest.

William stood straight and tall. He was determined not to leave this earth begging and pleading. He would show Legaic how a Christian dies.■

8

Small Steps Forward

The knife continued on its downward path, and William sent a quick prayer to Heaven to receive his soul. He shut his eyes and waited for Legaic's final thrust.

"Put your weapon down!" A commanding voice broke the silence. William opened his eyes as Clah stepped into the room, glaring menacingly at Legaic.

"I said drop your weapon," Clah repeated.

For a fleeting moment there was no movement, no sound. Then one by one the Indians left until only Legaic and Clah were left facing each other. Clah stepped forward, and Legaic shot a bitter, warning look at William and slunk out the door.

William sank down weakly on the nearest chair and tried to control his trembling hands. "My friend, what a lucky stroke that you happened to come along."

"It was not just luck," said Clah. "I have been observing the events of the last several hours. I would not let any harm come to you." He pulled his hand out from under his blanket. There was a gun in it.

William stared at the weapon. "I thank you for your friendship, but I pray that you will never have to use violence on my behalf. I do not wish to cause anyone any pain." Suddenly he jumped to his feet. "The children! Where are the children?"

He and Clah rushed outside and found the students huddled together under the schoolhouse.

"Come in now, youngsters. It is time to start class once more. There is no danger," said William.

"Legaic won't be back today," said Clah. "I shall leave now."

"Thank you again, my friend." William herded the children back into the building.

William was determined to put the scene out of his mind, and busily started to pass out books and papers and instruct his pupils. An hour passed, and the tension in the room was starting to dissolve.

"Now, we will learn a new song," said William. "Put your books . . ."

A loud thumping on the door interrupted him. Startled and apprehensive, William walked slowly across the room and opened the door a crack. Legaic pushed his way inside the room and looked at William defiantly.

The children! William could think of nothing but the children. Those innocents shouldn't see the spilling of blood. Angrily, he faced the Indian. "Why are you disturbing my class? Certainly you could have waited a few hours."

"This cannot wait," growled the Indian. "You think I am a bad man. I want to show you I am not. Look at these."

He handed William a package which contained two thin pieces of board, between which were some carefully arranged sheets of paper. William read the words on the paper, and felt his lips twitching as he tried to hide a smile. He had seen papers like this before. They were given to the Indians by Captain Lewis and other fort officials and were supposed to attest to their good character. Since most of the Indians couldn't read, these certificates, or "teapots" as the natives called them, were many times used as jokes. William had seen one that said, "This Indian is a no good, worthless loafer." The Indian to whom it had been given carried it proudly and showed it to everyone he saw.

William handed the certificate back to Legaic. "I don't have to read your 'teapot.' I know you better than the men who gave it to you. But that does not make any difference. I have no ill feeling against you. I have come here to make you good. Come in here and sit down and I will help make you better."

William took the chief's arm gently and tried to guide him to a chair. Legaic took a few steps, then grunted indignantly and hurried out the door.

William looked after the scurrying figure. He came to me in peace, he thought. Perhaps I can give in to his wishes this time and hold my classes in another village for a few days. We might each have to give a little in order to come to an understanding.

He turned back to his pupils with a feeling that he had taken a great step forward. Legaic had <u>almost</u> taken a seat in his schoolhouse.

Some days there were small steps forward. Other days William felt as if he was making no progress at all, but as the days grew colder and Christmas approached, William felt that he had a lot for which to be thankful. The number of both children and adults who attended school and church regularly was steadily increasing. Many of the Indians had become his close friends, and as he walked through the villages he was constantly greeted with smiles and outstretched hands.

In spite of this progress, he woke early Christmas morning with a strong sense of depression. He looked out his window and watched the swirling fog and the gray, choppy water in the bay. What is wrong with me? he wondered. Things are going well, I'm doing exactly what I want to be doing. It's Christmas, and my heart should be singing.

Then he knew—he was homesick for England and for his family and friends. He longed to taste Yorkshire pudding and goose and plum tarts, instead of fish and berries.

He dressed slowly, ate a quick breakfast, and walked to the schoolhouse to prepare for the holiday celebration. As he worked, the depression stayed with him and weighed him down.

That afternoon the Indians filled the schoolhouse and William fought to join in the holiday mood. He didn't want his gloom to spoil the feeling of Christmas. He picked up his concertina to accompany the singing, then looked down as he felt a slight tugging at his sleeve. A little girl, one of his youngest pupils, handed him some brightly colored seashells.

"These are for you," she whispered. "We love you."

Tears rushed into William's eyes and he blinked them back as he stroked the girl's smooth hair. As she went to her seat, he looked out upon the eager faces of his congregation. They were dressed in the shirts and dresses he had helped them buy from the company store. Their blankets were clean and their bodies free from the hideous yellow paint which many of them used to wear.

Why am I longing to be home? he thought wonderingly. This is my home. These are my people!

William noticed as the weeks went by that the hesitancy and shyness of the Indians had changed into willingness to talk and to exchange ideas with him. One day a group of chiefs came to his rooms. They stood looking at each other and then at William. After a few moments one of them cleared his throat. "If you wish, we have agreed to stop the eating of flesh in our ceremonies. We are also going to set aside some of our rituals. Our people seem to like

your church better than what the medicine men perform for them."

"I am pleased," said William. "All I do is repeat God's Word. He will be pleased also." He paused, then turned to one of the chiefs. "I would like to ask you one thing, though. I have been troubled since last Sunday when one of your tribesmen left the service early. He was muttering to himself as if he were angry about something I said or did. Could you tell me what reason I gave him for acting like that?"

The chief smiled. "Yes, I know the man. He drinks much liquor, and whenever you talk about the evils of alcohol, he thinks that you are talking directly to him. He says that you shame him in front of everyone."

"So that's it," said William. "You may tell him that I have never talked about any one person in my sermons. If he felt that I was talking about him, that means he knows he is doing something wrong."

The Indians nodded. "The shafts of your words are hitting many hearts," said one of them. "We are leaving for our summer fishing in a few weeks. We would like for you to keep speaking strongly against the bad ways of our people while we are gone. We will also support you by talking to other people while we are on our travels."

"This is good," said William. "God's Word should be spread far and wide."

William was teaching his class a few days later. Hands waved in the air in response to his questions, and voices were raised loudly and clearly as they sang hymns. William grew alert as Legaic entered and stomped to the back of the room, settled himself in a chair, folded his arms across his chest, and glared at him.

William felt himself relax. The chief was not threatening him. Instead, he seemed to be daring William to teach him something. William kept on with his class as though Legaic wasn't there. Every few minutes he glanced at the chief. Legaic sat straight and stiff, but his face was intent and his eyes observant.

The next day William prayed that Legaic would come back. When the chief appeared with four minor chieftains of his tribe, William wanted to shout with joy, but with an effort he simply continued quizzing his pupils and answering questions. The five men sat in the back of the room, not moving, but their eyes darted alertly about the room, and William was certain that everything he said was being recorded on their minds.

The days passed, then the weeks, and slowly the chiefs were no longer sitting in back of the room, isolated from the classroom proceedings. They had pulled their chairs forward, and their hands were raised constantly and their voices soared above those of the other students in their eagerness to sing and recite.

It's a miracle, thought William prayerfully. It's an example of how God can soften the hardest of hearts with His love. If He can speak so strongly to Legaic, who resisted His Word with all his might, I know that my mission is a succes.■

9

Fear Is Conquered at Last

One afternoon William was hurriedly preparing some pills for an Indian woman. He was worried about her because she had been seriously ill for over two weeks. He knew she was counting on his medicine to ease the pain in her stomach. It pleased him to think of how the natives had come to trust him. It pleased him even more when he realized that he had not seen a drunken Indian for almost a month.

As he put the pills in his bag, William smiled wryly. Not everyone was pleased about the growing temperance among the Indian tribes. Clah had told him that the white liquor traders had been complaining that they were losing too many customers.

William slammed the door after him. If it hadn't been for the white man's greed, he thought angrily, the Indians would never have started drinking alcohol in the first place.

As soon as he had left the gates of the fort, two Indians rushed out of the woods and fell to their knees in front of him. "Please, please, remain inside the walls of the fort," one of them pleaded. "Cushwaht is looking for you to kill you. He has already broken down the door of the schoolhouse and destroyed some books." He showed William a piece of wood. "See, here is a piece of the door which he broke into splinters."

William was bewildered. "Why is he so angry with me?"

"He has been bitten by a dog, and for some reason he blames you for his misfortune," the Indian replied.

William turned the piece of wood over and over. Finally he spoke. "My friends, I thank you for coming, but I promised to return to give this medicine to a very sick woman. She is in pain and is this moment awaiting my return. I cannot break my promise to her."

The other Indian grabbed William's arm. There were tears in his eyes. "Don't go! We do not want you to be killed."

William gently loosened his grip. "God will protect me as long as I am doing His work." He started to walk away.

"If Cushwaht kills you, we will kill him!" the first Indian shouted after him.

"I do not want any violence done on my behalf," William called back to them. "But I am grateful for your concern."

William had to walk right by Cushwaht's hut on the way to see the old woman. His heart was pounding and his legs trembled, but he forced himself to hold his head high and whistle carelessly. Out of the corner of his eye he saw a slight movement inside the hut, but he just whistled louder and kept walking.

A few minutes later he was entering his patient's hut. "Ah, here I am back again just as I promised," he said softly. "Soon you will be feeling better."

The woman swallowed the pills, then looked at him gratefully. "I was fearful that you would forget to come back. You have so much to do."

"I promised you, didn't . . ." William stopped. There was someone outside the hut. He tensed his muscles and prepared to defend himself.

The visitor was Cushwaht's wife. William looked at her warily, but she only sat and stared at him. He turned back to the patient. "Now you continue resting and I will be back tomorrow to see how you are." He arranged the blanket on top of her, picked up his bag, and started toward the door. To his surprise, he saw that Cushwaht's wife had slipped away and was already on her way back to her own hut.

Why was she there watching me like that? William wondered. Did Cushwaht send her? Then he remembered something Clah had once told him—that among the Indians a man who shows fear in the face of danger is scorned and is much more in danger of losing his life than someone who acts unafraid and unaware of danger. The reasoning was that a brave "spirit" would come out on top in any battle.

William grinned. It may have looked like he had a brave spirit on the outside. It was a good thing Cushwaht couldn't see how his spirit felt on the inside.

Two months later William was in his tent, which was pitched near the banks of the Nass River. As he watched his Indian guide sitting silently in front of the dying bonfire, he wondered if the old man had sensed his vague doubts about him.

This moment was one of the times that he wished he had listened to Captain Lewis. "You really mean to go that far away from the fort?" he had thundered. "At least here you have some chance of protection from those brown devils!"

William had been his usual stubborn self. He had been thinking for several weeks about visiting some of the outlying Tsimshian tribes, and since Clah had been willing to keep an eye on things at Port Simpson while he was gone, William had decided not to postpone the trip any longer.

He had followed the captain's advice up to a point, and had carefully chosen the natives who were to accompany him. The six young boys who were paddling the canoe had been his pupils ever since he had first started teaching. He knew that God had touched their hearts.

The guide had not been such a simple choice. He had to be an older man who knew the country well. All of the older Indians had been heathens all their lives, and while many of them were trying desperately hard to be good Christians, at times their old habits took over.

He had finally selected an older man who was not very strong. Although William trusted him, he knew that if anything happened he could overcome the Indian in a hand-to-hand fight.

Now as he lay looking at the old man, William felt uneasy. Why was the Indian just sitting there looking at the fire? What was on his mind as he puffed at his pipe? William knew that he couldn't go to sleep until the old man had gone to bed.

After almost an hour the Indian started spreading a thin bark mat on the ground. Then he arranged a few dry salmon to use for a pillow and spread his blanket out. When everything was ready, he put out his pipe and kneeled. Then in Tsimshian he began to pray, "Be merciful to me, Jesus."

The simple words brought tears to William's eyes. Forgive me for distrusting you, he said silently.

The following day William felt danger in the air as they drew close to the Tsimshian camp. His eyes were constantly on the river banks, looking for movement, for some sign that they were being watched.

Suddenly, as they rounded a bend in the river, he spied a tall Indian, dressed in chieftain's robes. He stood on the bank, waving and calling to them.

"Keep paddling," William said to the boys. "This may be a trick."

The old guide looked at the man for a few moments, then shook his head. "I do not think he is angry with you. I can tell by his attitude. Let us see what he wants."

William wished he could be that certain, but he told the boys to row close to the shore. As they drew near, he kept expecting to see a whole tribe of wild natives, dressed in war paint and waving their spears, appear from behind the trees.

"Greetings," his guide called. "We come from Port Simpson."

The chief waved. "I am Chief Kintsadah. I have come to guide you through the rapids. My people do not wish anything to harm you. Since the news of your visit reached our ears, we have been eagerly awaiting your message."

At a signal from the guide the boys paddled to the shore and the chief climbed into the boat. They sped down the river, and as the water started to swirl and eddy about them William knew they could have drowned without the expert guidance of someone who knew the river well.

Would these people forgive me if they knew the doubts I have about them? I came here to teach, and I am constantly finding that it is I who am being taught.

After almost an hour of travel the village came into view. Several Indians came down to the shore to help beach the canoe, and eager hands reached out to help William step out onto the sand. Kintsadah walked straight and tall beside him as they walked toward the cluster of huts.

"We have arranged a great dance in your honor—a big celebration," the chief announced proudly.

William was dismayed. He knew what the Indian dances were like—wild, devilish gyrations, with naked men in grotesque paint. He had come to preach a solemn message, not to watch a pagan ceremony. But could he afford to offend anyone?

He decided to chance it. "I cannot dance, or even watch a dance. What I have come to talk about is too important."

Kintsadah frowned. "I am afraid that if you do not watch the dance of the people, they will not be interested in hearing your message."

William considered his alternatives. If the Indians refused to listen to what he had to say, he had come all this way for nothing. On the other hand, could he let himself be part of a pagan ceremony?

He sighed. I'll have to compromise again. In order to take a step ahead, why must I so often have to take a step backward?

He was led to their meeting house. When he entered, he saw that they had prepared a special place for him to sit—a large box with a fur spread over it. There was a curtain separating one end of the building from the spectators. They had obviously taken much time to arrange the performance for William.

He took his place and tried to ignore his feeling of uneasiness. After all, if the dance became too wild and devilish he could always excuse himself and leave. Of course, then he might have to return to Port Simpson without telling this tribe of God's love.

The curtain was pulled aside, and he braced himself. There was a row of Indians standing on a crude stage. They were silent for a moment, then to William's astonished ears came a chant that sounded like the most beautiful of hymns.

"Pity us, Great Father in heaven, pity us. Give us Thy Good Book to do us good, and clear away our sins. This chief has come to tell us about Thee. It is good, Great Father. We want to hear. We will obey."

Then the chief gave a welcoming speech and the audience settled back expectantly as they waited for William to begin his sermon.

William could not move for several moments. How he had underestimated these people! Their "dance" was an invitation for God to be with them and fill their hearts.

William stayed with the tribe for several days. They learned Christian hymns and discussed the dangers of drinking alcoholic beverages. On the day he was to leave, a large group of young men came to him and asked him to write out a temperance pledge which they could sign.

When he had finished writing it, they each proudly placed their mark upon it, then folded the paper carefully and took it with them. William knew they would be showing their written pledge with pride and repeating his warnings long after he had left.

Then it was time to leave. In a flurry of farewells William left his new friends. As the canoe pulled away from the shore, he felt as if he were leaving a part of himself with them.

Oh, I wish we could all be together—live like brothers and sisters in one community, he thought. To be separated from parts of my family here is worse than being away from my other family in England.

As the strong arms of the Indian boys guided the canoe along the river, William made up his mind about one thing. He was no longer going to live behind the walls of the fort. As soon as he returned he was going to start building a cabin for himself in one of the Indian villages.■

10

A New Home: Metlakatla

True to his vow, William started building his cabin among the Indians as soon as he returned to Port Simpson. To his surprise Captain Lewis didn't try to talk him out of it.

"I throw up my hands," said the captain. "You are the most stubborn man I ever met."

"I know," said William. "If I weren't, I would have been back in England long ago."

Small but alarming incidents still occurred once in a while, reminding William that although some of the Indians were his trusted friends, many of them still disliked his intrusion into their lives. The most ordinary occasions could suddenly turn into a threatening situation.

One blustery fall day William was watching some Indian youngsters frolicking in a play area which he had set up for them. Several of them were standing in line waiting patiently for their turn to climb up a greased pole. A chill wind was blowing, and they were starting to shiver in their thin shirts.

"Here, you children, you should be running and getting warm. Run after me. The one who catches me first will win a piece of soap as a prize."

Laughing and shouting, the children started toward him. One of the younger boys stumbled and fell, and his laughter changed to a startled wail. Two girls standing nearby giggled when they saw he wasn't really hurt.

William rushed over to pick the boy up. "There, there, you aren't hurt. It's all right," he crooned.

Suddenly there was a commotion among a group of men and women who were watching. William put the child down and walked over to see what was happening. He stopped short when he saw a man with a gun aimed straight at his heart. It was Loocoal, a medicine man who had resented William's interference with the tribal ceremonies.

"You have shamed my child!" shouted Loocoal. "If he had not been running after you, he would not have fallen and been laughed at."

William felt himself grow limp as he stared unbelieving at the muzzle of the gun. Just seconds ago he had been sharing in the laughter and fun of the children. Now in another few seconds he might be dead.

Then before William realized what was happening, a man ran toward Loocoal and pushed the gun toward the ground. He was quickly joined by three other men who held the struggling medicine man until he dropped the weapon.

For a fleeting moment William thought of the security the fortress walls offered him. Then he looked down at the bright, questioning eyes of the children who had witnessed the scene. No, he decided, it is my business to spread the message of God among these people, so that these innocents will not ever have to see such violence again.

The schoolhouse, which had seemed so roomy when it had first been built, was rapidly becoming too small for the increasing

74

number of pupils. In the summer of 1861 still another building was started. Everyone who had not gone on the summer's fishing trip contributed time and effort. The men felled trees and cut logs and hoisted them into position. The children ran errands and cleared the area of brush. The women helped to earn money for materials by making baskets, spoons, and dishes and taking them to Victoria to sell.

The first trip to the city was such a success that they came back to make some more items to sell. After several such trips, an idea started growing in William's head. At first he tried to ignore it. It was too foolish, he told himself. It was impossible. His dreams were getting too big.

But the idea would not leave him. Every time he dwelled upon it, his heart beat a little faster and his imagination stretched further and further.

Finally he knew he had to share the idea with someone or he would certainly burst. He took Clah for a long walk in the woods one afternoon.

"I've been thinking," he said. "It seems to me that a good part of our problems come up because your people are constantly being tempted and duped by the white men—both the ones in the fort and the traders that they deal with. The white man is the one who supplies the Indian with liquor and defiles his women. The white men does not want your people to become educated and will do everything he can to stop me."

William paused and looked at Clah intently. "I have been thinking about forming a village far from here—a village where Christian natives could live together—away from scoffers among their own people and other bad influences, and where they could worship without the constant interference of the medicine men."

"It is indeed a wonderful idea," said Clah. "I will talk to some of the Christian chiefs and see what they think."

"You do not think me crazy for envisioning such a village?" asked William.

Clah laughed. "If it were anyone but you, I would think so. But I believe that when you make up your mind to do something, that thing will be done."

Encouraged by Clah and several chiefs who had accepted Jesus as their Savior, William brought up the subject of his Christian community to the entire congregation two weeks later.

"I have seen how you all worked together on the building of the schoolhouse," he concluded. "If we do the same in the building of our community, I know it will be a success. With your permission, some of the chiefs and I will start looking for a location immediately."

Within a few days everyone in the congregation had accepted the idea. The night before they were to start downriver to find a site, William knelt beside his bed and offered up a prayer of thanks.

"I know that it was You, O Lord, who planted this seed in my head and enabled it to grow. With Your guidance, the community will grow and flourish."

The search for the right location for the new village went on for several weeks. William and several Indians looked upriver for many fruitless days. Then they headed downstream. One morning they came upon an area which the Indians called Metlakatla. It was 17 miles south of Port Simpson. The minute William saw it, he knew this was the place for the village. In his mind's eye he could see rows of houses and a schoolhouse and a meetinghouse nestled among the trees. He turned to his companions and nodded. They nodded back in complete agreement.

That night in his cabin at the fort William thought of their new home with its protected harbor, fine beach, and the clearings where they would grow vegetables and flowers. He took up his pen and wrote in his journal: "It is a narrow, placid channel, studded with little promontories and pretty islands. A rich verdure, a waving forest, backed by lofty but densely wooded mountains. A solemn stillness, broken only by the cries of flocks of happy birds flying over, or by the more musical notes of some little warbler near at hand."

William and his congregation didn't want to waste a minute getting started on their new home. By May 14, 1862, they were ready to make the move. The schoolhouse had been dismantled and the materials piled on a large raft; a group of men had already started down the river with it. They were to go ahead and build a temporary shelter for William's books and medical supplies and plant some potatoes. William's heart had been full of happiness as he had watched them push away from shore. His dream was actually becoming a reality.

Two days later William was standing on the shore waving greetings to a group of men arriving in a canoe. The leader stepped out onto the beach. "I'm afraid I have bad news," he said. "We have just come from Victoria, and there is a smallpox epidemic there. Some of the men who started out with us in this boat died on the way here."

William examined the arrivals closely and with dismay noted the telltale spots of the disease on two of them. He immediately isolated the entire crew and cared for the sick men. As he worked he prayed for guidance. Should he abandon his plans to leave for the new village? The people here would need him if an epidemic struck. But what about the hopes and expectations of his congregation? For weeks they had talked about nothing but moving to their new home.

He decided to go ahead with his plans, but postponed the departure for several days while he instructed as many people as he could about how to treat smallpox. He wished he had been able to bring every person in all nine tribes to Jesus and to share God's love with all of them. Now he felt as if he were abandoning them to their fate. Twice he almost decided to stay and see them through the epidemic if it appeared, but each time he changed his mind when he thought of the Christian Indians who were depending on him.

Oh, why are there never any easy decisions? he wondered. Why do we always have to choose between two things we love?

William and part of his congregation pushed off from Port Simpson on May 27. His eyes filled with tears as he saw the huts disappearing in the distance. A part of his heart would always be with the ones who were staying behind. When he arrived at the new village he wrote:

> In the afternoon we started off. All that were ready to go with me occupied six canoes, and we numbered about 50 souls—men, women, and children. Many Indians were seated on the beach, watching our departure with solemn and anxious faces. Some promised to follow us within a few days. The party with me seemed filled with solemn joy as we pushed off, feeling that their long-looked-for flitting had actually commenced. I felt that we were beginning an eventful page in the history of these poor people, and earnestly sought God for His help and blessing.

When they arrived at the village site, William found that the advance party had been busy. They had already planted 50 bushels of potatoes and built two temporary shelters. That night the entire population sat on the beach singing, praying, and reading devotions. William felt a marvelous peace settle over him, and he saw the same peace on the faces of the Indians. This was meant to be, he decided. We have done the right thing.

The following morning William called them all together to present a list of rules he had drawn up.

"I know that what I am asking will not be easy for you," he said. "After all, I am asking for a complete break from your past. A halfhearted commitment will not do, because we cannot compromise with the devil. Here is what I will require of the ones who live here:

1. To give up Indian deviltry.
2. To cease calling on conjurers when sick.
3. To cease gambling.
4. To cease giving away property for display.
5. To cease painting your faces.
6. To cease drinking intoxicants.
7. To rest on the Sabbath.
8. To attend religious instruction.
9. To send your children to school.
10. To be clean.
11. To be industrious.
12. To be peaceful.
13. To be liberal and honest in trade.
14. To build neat houses.
15. To pay the village tax.

"If any of you feel you cannot make the sacrifices which I ask of you, you are free to return to Port Simpson and your old ways of life. I will have no ill feeling if you do. I do believe that the ones who stay will be opening their hearts to love, peace, joy, and prosperity."

When he had finished, William looked closely at the faces of his audience. He saw nothing but smiles and the nodding of heads. Yes, they would stay. They wanted what William had to give them.

On June 6th 30 more canoes arrived, carrying 300 people. Joyful shouts broke out when an entire tribe arrived along with its two chiefs.

The cheers quickly turned into sorrow when the newcomers reported that the smallpox plague had broken out in full force among the Indians at Port Simpson. More than 500 of them had already died from the ravages of the disease.

And it was such a short time ago that I spoke to them, thought William sadly. Now they have been suddenly swept away into eternity.

He turned and walked to his shelter. With an even heavier heart, he realized that he could expect smallpox to break out in his new village within the next few days.■

11

Legaic Comes to Metlakatla

Just as William had feared, smallpox struck the new community a few days later. In order to control it, he had the Indians put up a small infirmary and separated the patients from the rest of the natives. Every morning he checked everyone for signs of the disease. If anyone had a fever or skin eruption, he made his family stay away from him until he knew whether or not it was smallpox.

In spite of these precautions a great many Indians became ill. William worked day and night caring for them and comforting the grieving families. Because of his constant nursing only five patients died. One of these was a young man whom William had baptized just a few years earlier. He wrote sorrowfully of his death:

> He died in a most distressing condition . . . away from everyone he loved, in a little bark hut on a rocky beach, just beyond the reach of the tide, which no one of his relatives dared approach except the ones who nursed him. In this damp, lowly, distressing state how cheering to receive such words as the following from him:

I am quite happy. I find my Saviour is very dear to me. I am not afraid to die. I thank you, Mr. Duncan. I know that heaven is open to receive me. You told me of Jesus. I have hold of the ladder that reaches to heaven. I know that everything you taught me is true.

Do not weep for me. You are poor, being left. I am not poor. I am going to heaven. Be all of one heart and lie in peace.

As William had held his hand, he felt that all the work, the fears, and the doubts that had come from the time spent among these people had been worthwhile. The words which came from this one dying man had said everything he had wanted to hear.

William kept hoping that Legaic would someday join Metlakatla. He had often sensed that the chief was coming close to being converted, but then he would shy away and return to his heathen world. One day William was talking to Clah and the subject of Legaic's hesitation came up.

"Legaic may at some time accept Christ," said Clah, "but the thing that holds him back right now is that he would have to give up his chieftainship if he came with us."

"As much as I want Legaic here with us, I cannot compromise with him," said William. "We recognize no chiefs among us except those who excel in living upright Christian lives and show that they are true sons of God. I may lose Legaic forever. With so many chiefs leaving Port Simpson to come here, Legaic will be honored more than ever among the people who are left. He will be sought after for advice. At Metlakatla he would be as low as the lowest until his life showed that he was a true Christian."

William knew it would take a miracle to move Legaic's heart.

One cloudy morning William was overseeing the clearing of a plot of land when a canoe came down the river. He squinted, trying to make out who the arrivals were. Then his heart seemed to skip a beat. It couldn't be—but it was—there was Legaic and his whole family stepping onto the beach. Had the miracle William had prayed for really happened?

Legaic walked up to him as William forced himself to stand still instead of dancing for joy. "My family and I would like to join you in your new village. Smallpox has all but wiped out my tribe. God has indeed punished me for my pride. Please, let me join your people here."

William shook his head. "Our God is a kind, just God. He did not bring the plague upon your people to make you humble. But of course we will welcome you here."

As he walked toward the village with Legaic, William tried to ignore the small cloud that still hovered over him. If it was only fear that brought Legaic to Metlakatla, what would happen when he was no longer afraid?

Just as William had thought, Legaic was not wholly committed. For the next three months he was at Port Simpson as much as at Metlakatla. Every week he received a message saying that his presence was needed at a feast or at some sort of meeting or celebration. It was obvious to William that the Indians at Port Simpson did not want to lose Legaic to the Christians. They seemed to be playing a game of tug of war with him. Willim knew that eventually the chief would have to make a final decision, but he didn't want to force him to make a choice yet.

Then one evening Legaic came to William's cabin. He shifted uneasily from one foot to another and looked toward the ground as he spoke. "I must leave to attend another feast." William didn't say anything.

"Do you think I should go?" Legaic looked up. His eyes seemed to be asking William to tell him what to do.

"That is up to you," said William. "I cannot decide for you."

"But you don't approve, do you?"

"You are going to have to make up your own mind, but I will

say that you are soon going to have to decide one way or the other. Christians cannot compromise. You cannot serve both God and the devil. You cannot wear the mantle on both shoulders."

William hesitated. "While we are on the subject, there is something that concerns me. You do a lot of talking among the natives here about your attendance at these heathen ceremonies. If your heart is there with the heathen, then perhaps it is better that you leave here, for I cannot have the devil's work being done here at Metlakatla."

It had been extremely hard for William to say the words, because he felt that Legaic was truly trying as hard as he could. It was just that he didn't know where his heart really belonged.

Legaic stared at William for a few moments and the old hard expression reappeared on his face. Then he turned and left without saying another word. William opened his mouth to call him back. I know I can talk him into staying, he thought. Then he slumped wearily into a chair. No, he has to make up his own mind. It's no good if he stays just to please me. If his pride is more important than his God, then so be it.

An hour later William heard a commotion on the beach. He walked out of his cabin to see what was happening. Legaic had gathered his family together and was ready to leave. He stood beside the canoe shouting arrogantly, "I do not wish to stay here. I have many friends at Port Simpson and they have been calling to me. They tell me I am a great chief. Here I am nothing, so I choose to leave!"

As he started to push off into the water, the Indians knelt on the sand and prayed. William heard them asking God to speak to Legaic's heart. One of them saw William and ran toward him. "Please stop Legaic from leaving," he pleaded.

"I cannot stop him. I am the one who sent him away."

The natives looked bewildered. "You sent him away? But he is a head chief."

"It had to be done. He was doing the devil's work here."

The Indian returned to the group on the beach. A few seconds later they were all looking at William and muttering among themselves.

William was still deeply troubled three days later. He knew the Indians didn't understand what he had done. When he heard a knock on his door, he rose wearily to answer it. Legaic was standing there, his eyes glowing.

For a moment William didn't know whether to call for help or to welcome the chief in. "What is it you want?" he finally said uncertainly.

"I want to come in and talk with you." Legaic's voice was aggressive.

William stood aside and let him enter. The chief's shoulders were square and his back stiff. Suddenly he seemed to crumble and tears rand down his face.

"So you have come back," said William gently. "Why did you when I told you to go away?"

"Because I could not help it," said Legaic humbly. "I have not slept for three nights. I have come back to say to you—tell me what to do and I will do it. There is only one thing you must not tell me to do, for I will not do it."

"What is that?"

"Do not tell me to go away. I will not do that. I cannot do it."

William reached out and gripped Legaic's hands. He felt tears rush into his own eyes. He knew the wall between them was gone and it would never rise again.

Legaic became one of William's most willing workers. He helped the other Indians haul logs and put up roofs; by the time the first chill winds of autumn were blowing, 35 houses had been erected.

The Indians then decided that they wanted to build their

church before they did anything else. They were determined to have it done in time for Christmas. William insisted that the building be kept absolutely plain. He knew that the Indians were distracted too easily by ornaments and colorful decorations. He wanted his message to stand out, and not the objects surrounding it.

The completed building was a bare room which was large enough to hold 700 people. It had no flooring. The congregation sat on gravel. In the center there were two places to build roaring fires, and the smoke found its way upward and out through an opening in the center of the roof.

The Christmas services which were held in the new church were the most joyful William had ever seen. Everyone seemed to feel as he did—that now, at last, they were home.

At the beginning of the new year of 1863 a sense of well-being settled over Metlakatla. William was content when he wrote in his journal:

> About 400 to 600 souls attend divine services on Sundays. About 100 children are attending the day school and 100 adults the evening school.
>
> The instruments of the medicine men, which have spellbound their nation for ages, have found their way into my house, and are most willingly given up. The dark and cruel mantle of heathenism has been rent so it can never be made whole.
>
> Feasts are characterized by order and goodwill, and begin with the offering of thaks to the Giver of all gifts. Scarcely a soul remains away from divine service excepting the sick and their nurses. Evening family devotions are common in almost every house. Thus, the surrounding tribes now have a model village before them, acting as a powerful witness for the truth of the Gospel, shaming and correcting, yet still captivating them; for in it they see those good things which they and their forefathers have sought and laboured for in vain; to wit—peace, security, order, honesty, and progress. To God be all the praise and glory.

The Metlakatla Indians became known up and down the coast for their strict views on observing the Sabbath. When they went up the river to fish, they never threw out their nets on Sunday. One man was impressed with their sincerity:

> But what did the Christian Indians do when Sunday came? The first Sunday of their fishing season, although the fish had come up in greater abundance than ever and the season was so short, the Christians said, "We cannot go and fish."
>
> The heathen were full of excitement as they gathered in their fish, but the Christians said, "No, we are God's people. God will provide for us and we will spend the day as He tells us to do."

After the Indians had returned from their fishing, the man visited the Sunday worship service. He was tremendously moved:

> It was a strange, yet intensely interesting sight to see the countenance of the Indian; the tawny face, the high cheek bones, the glossy, jet black flowing hair, and the dark glossy eye, the manly brow were a picture worthy of the pencil of an artist.
>
> There were no external aids, sometimes thought necessary for the savage mind, to produce or increase the solemnity of the scene.
>
> The building was a mere barn. The roof was partly open at the top, and though the weather was cold, there was no fire. There was nothing to impress the senses, no colour or ornament, or church decoration or music. The solemn stillness was broken only by the breath of prayer. The responses were made with earnestness and decision. Not an individual was there whose lips did not utter, in their own expressive tongue, their hearty readiness to believe and to serve God.■

12

Independence

Observing the Sabbath was not always an easy thing to do. There was a constant need for money to but necessities which the new community couldn't provide for itself. One day a man named Captain Butler came to Metlakatla and asked William if he could hire some of the Indians. He worked for the Western Union Telegraph Company and was in a great hurry to get a shipment of wire and other materials to some of his workmen in the interior of Canada. These men would be sitting idle until the supplies reached them.

"Please let me hire some men," he pleaded. "The supplies must be rushed up the Skeena River."

"Certainly, you may have as many men as you want," said William. "They would be happy to do it. But remember, my men will not work on Sundays."

Captain Butler frowned. "That is too bad. We are in such a

hurry, and every day's delay means that we are losing a small fortune." Then he shrugged. "But never mind. Get me 24 men and four canoes anyway."

William quickly rearranged the work schedule of several natives, then went to Captain Butler to talk about the salary and length of employment.

"Oh, I'm sorry," the captain said when William told him his men were ready to start work. "I've already hired some other Indians who could work on Sunday."

William saw that the other Indians were tying their canoes onto the rear of the captain's small steamship. Evidently they were just about ready to start off.

William bit his tongue to hold back the angry words that flew into his mouth. He turned quickly and went back to tell his men the discouraging news.

The Indians were angrier than he was. "This is not right," said one of them stubbornly. "We have counted on earning that money. What can we do?"

William thought for a few moments. As he did, the familiar stubbornness stiffened his back. With a quick nod he replied, "He has hired you and he has insulted you by passing you by. You had better paddle your canoes until you catch up with the steamship. Then tell him that you are ready to go to work as it was agreed."

The men quickly got some food together and pushed off. As they disappeared from sight, William hoped he wasn't sending them off only to face another disappointment.

Two weeks later the men returned with smiles on their faces and money in their pockets. They laughed as they told William that Captain Butler had been overjoyed to see them. The other Indians he had hired had deserted him as soon as they had arrived at the loading dock.

"It seems that all they wanted was a free ride up the river," said one of the younger men.

90

"So we went right to work," he continued. "There were also some white sailors helping to load the supplies. We all started up the river with the loaded canoes on a Saturday morning. Of course, the next day was the Sabbath and we stopped and tied up our canoes and started to worship."

Another man broke in. "Captain Butler was very angry. He swore at us and he begged us and he offered us more money. Of course, we did not budge."

"Yes," another Indian said. "The white sailors taunted us and tried to shame us—calling us lazy and other names. We just ignored them, and they soon rowed away and left us.

"Monday morning we started out once again, and by Tuesday noon we had caught up with them. Soon we had passed them up, and then when we looked back we could not even see them."

The Indians roared with laughter as they told the story. William joined with them, all the time thinking how proud he was of his men.

A few weeks later Captain Butler came back to Metlakatla and asked William if he could hire some more Indians.

"I'm sorry for the way I treated them before," he said. "They were the best workers I've ever seen. Even not working Sundays they did more than the men who worked the entire seven days. With your permission I will be back often to hire them."

"Their performance does not surprise me," said William. "It is what I expect of them, and they never disappoint me."

The population of Metlakatla kept growing steadily. New colonists were admitted from Port Simpson and from outlying tribes. Every Christian who heard of the village wanted to live there. There were times when over 100 new members arrived all at once.

William was glad to see the growth, but he realized that other ways of supporting his people must be found. Just because a Tsimshian became a Christian did not mean that he became a better hunter or fisherman than he had been when he was a heathen. In fact, most of the time, while his income remained the same, his expenses rose. Instead of using one dirty old blanket to wrap himself in, he now had to buy clothes. His wife and children used to run around naked. Now they needed both work clothes and something to wear to church.

There must be more ways to make money, William thought. What we need is some small industries where the Indians can work and make money. But the problem was how to finance the beginnings of these industries. He was already using all of his small income from the missionary society to pay for the work the Indians did on his home and on the church. He had also paid them for putting in roads, drainage ditches, and for the building of a public house where visitors to the village could stay.

He decided to lay out 100 garden plots on a nearby island and give them to the villagers so they could raise potatoes to sell. He also instructed them to prepare smoked salmon, oolaken grease, and dried berries, and they took them to Victoria to sell along with some furs.

The Indians then built a soap factory, where they made inexpensive soap from oolaken grease. They had plenty for themselves, with enough left over to sell.

William was happy with the money that had started coming into the village. However, he found there was one problem. When the Indians wanted to buy clothes and tools with that money, they had to go to Port Simpson or to encourage the trading schooners to stop at Metlakatla. Every time the soldiers at the fort or the sailors on the ships saw the Indians they encouraged them to drink and to gamble. They also cheated them unmercifully in any business transaction.

In order to keep the contacts between the whites and the Indians down as much as possible, William tried to persuade the officials of the Hudson's Bay Company to open a post near Metlakatla. All he asked was that they charge fair prices, that no intoxicating beverages be sold, and that the agent in charge be a decent, honest man.

His request was refused, as he had half expected it would be. The Hudson's Bay Company had never liked William's interference with the way they wanted the Indians handled. William had encouraged the natives to become independent and to stand up for what they knew was right.

The officials went one step further and put pressure on the independent storekeepers so they wouldn't open any stores near Metlakatla.

The stumbling blocks which the Hudson's Bay Company put in his way only made William more determined. He decided to open his own store. He had put some money aside for an emergency. He used almost all of these savings to buy a small stock of supplies.

Then another problem arose. The Hudson's Bay Company owned all the steamers that sailed up and down the coast. Since Metlakatla was 600 miles from Victoria, which was the nearest source of supply outside of Port Simpson, he had to transport his stock on those ships. He was dismayed, but not surprised, when he found that the steamers had orders not to carry anything in or out of Metlakatla.

All right, he thought, I'll have to buy my own steamer. But how? His money was almost gone. In desperation he wrote to the governor of the province and asked to borrow $500. To raise the rest of the purchase price he asked the Indians to buy shares in the ship at $5.00 apiece.

He wasn't sure they understood what they were doing when they handed him their money, but he collected enough to pay for the small steamer.

The Indians quickly learned how to operate the ship, and the entire village gathered on the dock and watched as it started on its first trip to Victoria. There were loud cheers as it chugged down the coast.

Thank goodness, William thought. Our troubles with the Hudson's Bay Company are over.

The steamer, which they had named the <u>Caroline,</u> made constant trips up and down the coast, bringing supplies from Victoria and carrying the products of the Indians to the city. As soon as the other tribes found they could get three to four dollars for their martens instead of the 25 cents the Hudson's Bay Company paid, or 75 cents instead of two cents for minks, they brought all their furs to Metlakatla.

At the close of the first year of trading William called the shareholders together and paid each of them a five dollar dividend. They all tried to give him the money back.

"No, no we will not take it," they protested.

"Why?" William asked in amazement.

"We want to keep our share of the <u>Caroline.</u>"

William laughed. "I understand. But you see, this is your share of the profits. You still own your share."

"You mean we get five dollars for doing nothing?" one man cried. "This is indeed wonderful. We must rename the ship <u>Hah</u>, which means slave, for he does all the work and we get all the profits."

The Hudson's Bay officials were not going to stand by and let William ruin their business. They put out an order to overbid William on furs and to undersell him on goods that the Indians needed. Even if they lost money, they were determined to crush William's growing business.

William had been expecting that they would start fighting back. He already had a plan which would discourage them. He went to Port Simpson to talk to Captain Lewis:

I will tell you frankly how I intend to act in this matter. Then you can take your measures accordingly. . . . The moment I find that you raise the price of furs above a fair profit, or lower the price of goods below a fair profit, I will not sell another article. I will send the Indians to you and tell them they can make a good profit by coming to the fort. But, mind you, you will have to keep on with your plan and your prices. For the moment I learn that you have come down on the furs or have come up on your store goods, I will tell the Indians to come and trade with me once more.

Captain Lewis swore and blustered and ranted. He knew that there was nothing he could do to outwit William. Within a week the orders had been revoked. Everyone at the fort knew that this was the first time in the history of the Company that it had been defeated, and it had been done by a destitute missionary and his poverty-stricken congregation.

Within a few months William had repaid all of the $500 he had borrowed from the governor. A short while later William received a letter from him. The letter told of the governor's amazement and gratitude: "I had not thought that my 'loan' was anything but a donation to the village of Metlakatla. No missionary has ever repaid me before, and I had not expected it from you."

William reread the letter with a warm feeling of satisfaction. It wasn't just I who repaid the money, he thought. It was the people of my village.■

13

Life at Metlakatla

By the spring of 1864 the village was running so smoothly that William and Clah decided to go back to Port Simpson for a visit. Many of the Indians had chosen not to move to Metlakatla, but William did not want to forget the ones who were left behind.

At the last minute Legaic asked if he could go with them. William looked at him inquiringly.

Legaic grinned. "I do not wish to stay at Port Simpson. My chieftainship means nothing to me now. But perhaps I can be of some help to you there."

William nodded. "Yes, perhaps you can. Go and collect the things you need to take with you."

On the second day of the visit to Port Simpson, William and Legaic and a group of natives were sitting around a bonfire on the beach in the early evening. William was glad they had made the trip. It seemed to him that several of the Indians were thinking seriously about coming to join the group at Metlakatla. Out of the corner of his eye he looked at one old Indian who seemed to have something on his mind. He had opened his mouth to speak several times, but then had sat back and remained silent.

During a lull in the conversation the old Indian suddenly stood up and looked at William accusingly. "You should have come much sooner to be among us," he growled. "You should have been here when the white traders first came. Then we would not have been infected with their sins of drunkenness and gambling. Now our sins are so deep that we can never change."

William opened his mouth to reply when suddenly Legaic leaped to his feet. "I am a chief, a Tsimshian chief," he said clearly. "You know I have been bad, as bad as many here. I have grown up and grown old in sin. But God has changed my heart, and He can change yours. Think not to excuse yourself in your sins by saying you are too old, or too bad, to mend. Nothing is impossible with God. Come to God. Try His way. He can save you."

Legaic has said it all, thought William. There is nothing I can add. This is the man who once tried to kill me—the man I almost gave up on. Now in these few words he has preached a sermon much better than any of mine.

When William returned to Metlakatla he threw himself into the projects he had been thinking about while he was on the trip. Within a few months the village was a beehive of activity. The trading store was constantly busy, and the profits from it were applied to building houses, pathways, and roads, and to hiring people to train the Indians in a variety of crafts and trades. Small businesses were established, many of which could be carried on right in the individual homes.

A blacksmith shop and a carpentry shop were built. When William discovered some clay nearby, he had a kiln built and the Indians went into the brickmaking business.

It soon became obvious that much more work could be done

if the workers didn't have to depend only upon their own backs and shoulders for power. William decided to make use of the great abundance of water in the streams just outside the village. He showed the natives how to build a water wheel and how to transform the push of the rushing water into energy which could do much of their work.

This energy was soon put to use in a sawmill. On the first day of its operation William noticed that one of the natives seemed especially captivated by the machinery in operation. He had been watching the wood cutting for hours.

William walked up to him. "That is going to make our work much easier."

The Indian turned to him, his eye filled with awe. "I want to die now," he said.

William stared at him. "Why do you say that?"

"I want to go and meet our old chiefs and tell them the wonder I have seen, that you have made water saw wood. They never heard or saw anything like that while they lived, and I want to be the first one to tell them."

Many of the Indians at Metlakatla were now able to read and write. William decided that it was time to give them a share in governing the village. He first appointed a council who advised him in all community affairs. Then he appointed a board of elders for the church.

As they learned more about government, general elections were held and the natives chose their own council and board of elders.

William was constantly impressed by the high quality of the men they placed in office. After one election, however, he was puzzled by one of their choices for the board of elders. The newly elected man had won by a high majority. His name was Silas, and the only thing William knew about him was that he was a very quiet, even-tempered man. He had never contributed much to the church services outside of what everyone was expected to do. He asked Clah what he knew about Silas.

"You do not really know him," replied Clah. "He is quiet here, but when he is at the fishing stations on Sundays, he always gathers the people around him and prays, speaks, exhorts, and does a great work. Greater than any one of us."

The people of the village are constantly proving that they are wise, thought William. Indeed, many of them know much more than I ever will.

At the next council election William was puzzled again. There had been one vote cast against a candidate whom William had always thought of as being honest, upright, and dedicated to the good of the community. One vote didn't mean that he couldn't serve, but William wondered if someone had voted against him by mistake. He arranged another election. Again there was one dissenting vote. Perhaps someone has voted out of spite or some personal grievance, thought William.

He wanted to keep the election ballots secret, but he was concerned as to whether some people voted for or against a man for the wrong reasons. He knew that democracy would work best if people could overcome their personal feelings about a man and vote only for the good of the church or community.

He went through the village and let everyone know that he would like to talk in confidence to the one who had voted against the man. The next morning before dawn he heard someone walking around his house. He looked out the window.

"What do you want?" he called softly.

"I am the man who voted nay in yesterday's election," the visitor whispered.

William rushed to the front door and let the Indian in. "Thank you for coming," he said. "I don't want to pry, but I must know what prompted you to vote as you did. If you did the man a disservice, it should be corrected. I suppose you had grounds for your dissenting vote?"

"I will tell you, and you can judge for yourself. He and I were at the store together one day. He paid for some goods. By mistake he got one dollar too much in change. After a while he showed it to me and asked me if he should give it back to the storekeeper or keep it. I told him to give it back. And he did. But I thought that a man who did not know enough to be honest in the first place was not fit to be elder of the church."

"You are right," said William. "Thank you for telling me."

The democracy at Metlakatla will work, thought William. How can it not work with this sort of thinking?

As more and more people moved to the village, it was inevitable that there would be a few troublemakers. William welcomed everyone, and if some of them had a few problems adjusting to the ways of the community, he always took the time to counsel them. Almost everyone eventually became a good contributing member of the community.

But there were a few who, after all the efforts of William and the council, just didn't fit in. Newcomers who disrupted the routine of living, who caused unhappiness among the established citizens, or who wouldn't do their share of the work had to leave.

William didn't like to give a direct eviction order because he knew how the Indians felt about being shamed. Instead, if the individual hadn't stopped his troublemaking after a final warning from William, a black flag was run up on the flagpole. That way the unwanted Indian had an opportunity to leave of his own accord. He would not be shamed in the eyes of his friends.

If he still didn't leave and persisted in disrupting the village, public pressure was used. By then most people knew who the black flag had been run up for. Cold stares and cold shoulders usually drove the troublemaker out of the community within a few days.

William never gave up on the men who had been forced out of the village. He had so often found that even the worst of men could change if they wanted to. One day he was in Victoria when he heard that Cushwaht, his sworn enemy, had been arrested and was in the

100

city jail. He had been drunk and had shot at a white sailor.

William visited Cushwaht in his cell. After a long talk he sensed that the Indian was truly sorry for the life he had been leading. Almost against his better judgment, William talked the judge into releasing Cushwaht, saying that he himself would see to it that the prisoner stayed out of trouble.

William told Cushwaht to return to Port Simpson and to stop drinking and to make every effort to lead a nonviolent life.

Cushwaht clasped William's hand. "No man has ever done such a thing for me before. I promise you that you shall never find fault with me again."

William kept in touch with Cushwaht's wife every few weeks. At the first sign of trouble he was prepared to go to Port Simpson and confront the Indian. The trip was never necessary. Every report showed steady progress. Then Cushwaht started attending church services near the fort. As far as William knew, his former enemy was never again in any trouble.

If only my problems with the white men were so easily solved, thought William one day. He was standing at the dock at Metlakatla as the anchor of a Russian schooner slid into the water.

William had heard that there was liquor on board, and he wanted to ward off trouble before it got started. He boarded the ship and confronted the captain with his suspicions.

"I have no objection to your trading here," he said. "But I can allow no liquor to be brought onto the shore."

"Oh, but I have none on board," the captain said.

"I have heard differently," replied William. "In order to ease my mind, I must search your ship."

The captain looked at him coldly. "What authority do you have for such a request?"

"Authority? I have no authority, sir, except the authority of self-defense. My life is in the hands of these Indians. They are my friends now. But if you take away their reason with liquor, I will have nothing to defend my life with. And I am going to prevent you from placing my life in jeopardy, if I can."

The captain grudgingly allowed William to search the ship. He didn't find any liquor. It's no doubt well hidden, William decided. I'll just have to watch the trading operation closely. Then he will not be able to pass anything along to the Indians.

The captain gave him a stony look as he left, but didn't say anything else. The trading was completed quickly, and the ship sailed off toward Victoria.

Three weeks later William received a letter from the governor of British Columbia. "Captain Baranovitch came to me complaining of your highhanded treatment of a peaceful trading vessel," wrote the governor. "However, instead of censuring you for taking the law into your own hands, I am now giving you legal authority to protect yourself. I have appointed you justice of the peace with jurisdiction over 500 miles of the coastline of British Columbia and over the islands which lie nearby."

William reached for a pen and paper so he could thank the governor for the appointment. He smiled to himself as he wondered whether anyone else had ever been made a justice of the peace by breaking the law.■

14

William Goes Home

William was able to handle his new office because the Indians were becoming more and more capable of handling the everyday affairs of the village. Besides that, the Missionary Society had sent several young missionaries and their wives to help out at Metlakatla. While the men helped with the heavier work, their wives trained classes of Indian girls in sewing, cooking, and housekeeping. As the Indian men married these girls, they set up well-run Christian households.

Indian men, as they learned to read and write, had been taking over the teaching of Bible classes. Metlakatla was becoming what William had originally envisioned—"a brilliant beacon light on the desolate northwest coasts, sending its splendid rays in all directions, the guiding star of the heathen tribes, towards the only port of safety and happiness on a rocky and dangerous coast."

However, William was still not completely content. He wrote in his journal one evening:

The sources of industry at present in the hands of the Indians are too limited and inadequate to enable them to meet their increased expenditures as a Christian and civilized community . . . . Numbers of young men are growing up in the mission who want work, and work must be found for them, or mischief will follow. They will be drawn to the settlements of the Whites, where numbers of them will be sure to become the victims of the white man's vices and diseases.

There was just one solution. He had to make a trip to England, where he could learn about new trades which he would be able to teach the Indians. In 1870 he decided the time was right for such a trip. The elders were able to handle the church programs. The constables had the necessary experience to maintain order. The village council knew what was expected of it. There was a competent storekeeper in charge of the store. William knew that the schooling and industry of the village would continue in his absence.

There would be an added bonus to his trip. It would show the natives that he trusted them to run their own affairs.

He left in January after saying good-bye to everyone in the village. Crowds gathered on the beach to wave to him. Several men jumped into their canoes and followed his ship down the coast until they had to turn back.

When he arrived in his hometown of Beverley, he spent several days visiting friends and relatives. He had a joyful reunion with his mother, who kept exclaiming over the lines in his face and his full beard.

He wished he had more time, but within a week he felt he should be going about his business. To start off, he visited with an old Irish woman who taught him how to spin wool. Then he went to Manchester to learn weaving and carding, to Yarmouth for ropemaking. Then without a day's rest he went to other nearby towns to learn barrel making and shoemaking.

He filled dozens of notebooks with notes so he wouldn't forget what he was learning. When he passed a photographer's shop, he stopped on impulse and asked about learning that trade. By the time he was through he had bought a camera and developing materials to take back to Canada with him.

He also wanted to buy some musical instruments. The natives had a good ear for music, and he had always wanted to organize a brass band at Metlakatla. He found a man who had bought some instruments but found he had no use for them. William told him about the Indians and what they had accomplished. Then he told him about his dreams of a band.

When he had finished talking, the man said gruffly, "My instruments are not for sale, sir."

"All right," said William, "I beg your pardon for intruding and taking up your time."

"I said they were not for sale. But that does not prevent my making you a present of them, does it? You may take them. I hope you will have joy from them."

William felt that God must have led him directly to this man.

He gathered his purchases and notes together and went to San Francisco, where he bought a set of looms and other weaving equipment. Then he hurried to Victoria, where he located a music teacher.

"I have bought 30 instruments and intend to organize a band," he told him. "I must learn how to play them."

The teacher's eyes widened in surprise.

"And I have only a limited time," William continued.

"How much time have you?" asked the teacher.

"I leave here in eight days for the north."

The teacher looked as if he were going to faint but, undaunted, said he would try. Every day and far into the night they worked together constantly. When the time was up, William knew enough about each instrument to be able to teach the Indians the basics.

The news of his arrival traveled ahead of him, and when he arrived at the mouth of the Skeena a group of Indians met him with a large canoe. William left the steamer and traveled the rest of the way with them. It seemed as if no one could stop talking long enough to let anyone else speak. As William listened to the excited babble of voices, he was overwhelmed with the happines he felt at being home again.

When the canoe was beached near the village, the sand was crowded with men, women, and children. As William stepped out onto the beach, the babble of conversation became a torrent of sound. William later wrote: "The Indians poured out one piece of news after another in rapid succession and without any regard to order, or the changes their reports had on my feelings. Thus we had good and bad, solemn and frivolous news, all mixed indiscriminately."

The welcoming celebration was almost more than William could take. The village had been decorated with flags. Cannons went off, one after another, and the constable corps fired muskets in the air. Everyone threw hats in the air over and over, and tears and smiles covered everyone's face.

As William walked to the Mission House, the Indians reached for him and crowded around him. Soon his tears were mingling with theirs. The children were lined up in front of the Mission House. William broke down completely when he saw their small hands raised in greeting.

William entered his small front room, and the knowledge of how much he had missed his village swept over him and left him weak. Gulping back his tears, he placed his baggage on his bed and went back outside.

A church service had been arranged. After he had thanked God for his safe return, the crowds continued to follow him as he visited with the sick and the elderly who were too feeble to leave their homes. Then everyone gathered in front of the Mission House until midnight singing and praying and talking. William heard some of the natives celebrating long after he had fallen into bed, exhausted but filled with joy.

The next day he wrote:

> I could not help but reflect how different this was from the reception I had among the same people in 1857. It was with fear and

contempt they approached me to hear God's Word, and when I prayed among them I prayed alone. None understood.

Now how things have changed! Love has taken the place of fear, and light the place of darkness, and hundreds are able and willing to join me in prayer and praise to Almighty God.

Within a few days William plunged back into the routine of the village. At the same time he was trying to review what had happened while he was gone. He was pleased with the way the constables had handled the discipline. There was only one case where he would have decided differently from the way they did.

William wasted no time in establishing some of the new industries he had learned. Soon the Indians were making shoes, barrels, doors, and rope walks for sale.

The weaving industry turned out to be one of the most successful. Metlakatla shawls fast became famous up and down the coast for their durability.

The band was formed, and at first the woods rang with terrible noises. But slowly the Indians learned how to play their instruments and the noise turned into music. Later William hired a musician to stay at the village for three months to work with the band members.

Under William's direction every house in the village was strengthened and repaired. The older temporary dwellings were torn down and replaced with sturdy two story houses with chimneys and windows. Every yard was neatly fenced in and had flowers and berries growing in the front, and vegetables in the back.

Within a few months work had been started on a large, new church which would hold 1,200 people, and after it was done a two story schoolhouse was built. It held 800 students and contained an auditorium.

From time to time a starved, naked Indian stumbled in through the gates of Metlakatla. These were men who had been kept in slavery by some of the coastal tribes. They had heard of William and had escaped and fled to him for shelter. The minute a slave reached the village, he was free forever. If his owners came after him, William confronted them and told them that he would

never hand any man over to them.

As the money built up in the village treasury, William started to visit these tribes and buy freedom for the remaining slaves. He brought them back to Metlakatla, where they were sheltered and clothed and fed. Most of them became some of the congregation's most ardent and hardworking Christians.

William kept busy all day and into the night. He was preacher, schoolmaster, doctor, magistrate, chief of police, mayor, store manager, overseer of the sawmill and half a dozen other businesses, bookkeeper, and adviser and arbitrator for 1,000 people.

And every night he thanked God for giving him the opportunity to do all these things.■

15

Practicing What Is Preached

As if he didn't have enough to do, William's interests started extending outside the borders of Metlaktla. In 1875 he made a trip to Ottawa to protest the attempts of white speculators to take away the Indians' land. These speculators were forcing the natives to give up wide stretches of their ancestral hunting and fishing grounds. The Indians were already poor. If they lost their land, they would be in danger of starving to death.

William didn't think the Indians were going to give up their land without a fight. He could foresee warfare and slaughter if he failed to convince the government officials to step in.

He had long talks with Lord Dufferin, the Governor-General of the Dominion. When William told him what he had done at Metlakatla, the official asked question after question and seemed amazed that he had never heard of the village before.

As William left, Lord Dufferin shook his hand and smiled

warmly. "I shall certainly help you in your just fight to save the land for the Indians," he said. "And I hope I shall see you once again."

Exactly one year later William looked up from directing some work at the sawmill and saw a boat coming. It pulled up to the shore, and Lord Dufferin and his wife stepped out. William blinked and looked again. It was really they. He told the Indians to stop their work and prepare a banquet in honor of their guests.

During the next few days the official saw with his own eyes how the Tsimshians were progressing under William's guidance.

"This is a miracle," he said when he left. "And I am doing everything within my power to correct the problem we talked about last year."

"Thank you," said William, "and I know the Indians will bless your name."

A few weeks later Captain Prevost also paid Metlakatla a visit. He shook his head in disbelief as he saw what William had done. He wrote to the Missionary Society that night: ". . . having once known their former lives, I know that the love of God . . . can alone have produced such a marvelous change."

The village continued to grow and prosper, and William sent up prayers of thanks every night. Whenever he saw the bright-eyed, healthy children bending over their books in the classroom, he felt as if he would burst with happiness. When he met with the board of elders of the council, he knew that the Indians were as proud of their village as he was.

The peace and happiness which he felt were disturbed in November of 1879. Rev. William Ridley had been appointed as bishop of William's diocese, and he immediately told William that he was going to make Metlakatla his episcopal seat.

As William watched the bishop bustle around in his regal-looking robes, little warnings fluttered inside of him. What would happen to the plain, simple services the Indians had grown accustomed to? Would the bare walls of the church now be covered with ornaments and distracting statuary? What effect would these changes have on the Indians?

Bishop Ridley reassured William that nothing would be changed. He kept repeating that he had only admiration for the work that had been done at Metlakatla.

Why can't I believe him? wondered William. Could it be that my pride has been wounded? After all, I am only a lay missionary with no titles or official standing.

On the other hand he knew that he understood the Tsimshians much more than Bishop Ridley did. The bishop had no idea of how to speak their language or of how they behaved or thought.

The bishop asked William some unsettling questions. "Are all the members of your congregation baptized?" he asked one day.

"No," said William. "I do not take Baptism lightly, and I don't want anyone baptized until I am convinced that he knows what significance such a step has. I heard of one preacher who boasted of baptizing '500 bloodthirsty savages' just a few days after meeting with them. I cannot believe that those 'savages' knew what they were doing."

The bishop frowned.

William had the feeling he didn't agree with the way anything had been done at Metlakatla, but for now he would just have to wait and see. If the bishop confronted him, William hoped that he would be able to show him the reasons behind the things he did.

As the weeks went on, William realized that Bishop Ridley was not going to confront him openly. Instead, there was a slow, constant undermining of William's authority. Men were taken from jobs to which William had assigned them and put in places where they couldn't do anything. Missions were erected in locations where they weren't needed and staffed with people who knew nothing about the Tsimshians. Bishop Ridley took some of William's most dependable natives and sent them to these missions to do menial work.

The situation continued to worsen, and William knew that there would be open conflict between himself and Bishop Ridley. He knew the effect such a conflict might have on the Indians. At the next Northwest Coast Mission conference he offered to resign. Then he left the room so the delegates would not feel any pressure as they made their decision.

He paced the floor outside the meeting room, wondering if he had done the right thing. Was he deserting his congregation? Was he being selfish and thinking only of his wounded pride?

"O Lord, please help me to do the right thing," he murmured distractedly.

Although he tried to push the thought out of his mind, he couldn't help reflecting on the fact that it was again a white man who stood between him and his goals. His place was with the Indians—struggling alongside them toward a better life and an understanding of God's love. What if they accept my resignation? he agonized. How can I leave my people?

After what seemed an eternity, William was summoned back into the meeting room. The leader read from his notes: "The conference, having heard Mr. Duncan's statement, and knowing the value of his labors and experience, not only in the work at Metlakatla but also to the Church Missionary Society's missions generally in the North Pacific field, unanimously decline to advise Mr. Duncan to resign."

William felt weak as the tension left him. Then he gathered himself up. He couldn't leave the situation in the air or nothing would improve.

"I am being asked to make changes at Metlakatla which I cannot endorse," he announced. "I respectfully ask whether you could advise the Society to allow the village to become

113

independent as long as it doesn't interfere with any other missions or missionaries."

Without any hesitation the conference passed a resolution to advise the Society to do as William requested.

William returned to Metlakatla knowing that his first meeting with Bishop Ridley would probably be a stormy one. He was right. The bishop looked at him with disgust.

"The conference's action is absurd and cowardly," he said coldly and then walked haughtily away.

William felt as if he couldn't waste any time on his opponent's wounded feelings. He had work to do. He had to go to Victoria to get machinery for a salmon processing plant which would enable the Indians to make more of a profit from the fish they caught. While he was still in the city, he received an invitation from the Missionary Society in England to come and discuss the future of Metlakatla with them. He immediately wrote and told them that he would have to postpone the trip until the processing plant was running smoothly.

He didn't think any more about the matter until he returned to the village. Bishop Ridley was waiting for him on the beach with a triumphant expression on his face.

"Are you going to England?" he asked.

"No," replied William, "I will go later if they wish."

With a flourish the bishop produced a letter. "There," he said, "I guess I am master now!"

William numbly opened the letter. It was addressed to the bishop and said that if William refused to come to England immediately, his relationship with Metlakatla was over and Bishop Ridley was to take charge.

William felt as if he were having a nightmare. "I—I don't understand," he stammered. He glanced at the date on the letter. It had been sent on the same date as the letter he received in Victoria! That letter had seemed to be only an invitation, which he could accept or refuse. It had never given any hint of the consequences if he didn't leave immediately for England.

Somewhere along the line there had been a terrible confusion, and William had been trapped in it. Bishop Ridley had won. William stood silently, too stunned to speak. Had all of his years among his beloved friends been for nothing?

As soon as he felt able, William started to remove his clothes and books from his cabin. Word of what had happened spread like wildfire, and the Indians immediately prepared a small house where William could stay until his final departure. Hundreds of natives appeared from every corner of the village to help him move his belongings. William's heart ached at the thought of being separated from them forever.

While William made his preparations to leave, the Indians had a series of meetings. After each one, they came to William and begged him to stay and go on teaching them.

"No," William said over and over, "you will be all right without me. I do not want to cause any trouble or unrest by my presence."

Oh, my friends, he thought silently, if you only knew how it pains me to say these words.

Finally there was one tremendous meeting. Every Indian in the village attended—the sick, the crippled, the young, and the aged. They begged William to attend, but he said it would be better if he continued with his packing.

Later that evening a delegation came to William's door. "We know what we owe you," said the spokesman. "Happy homes, loving families, peace, order, prosperity here on earth, and a hope of going to heaven. Every one of us voted to ask you to please stay with us."

Tears blurred William's vision. He tried to refuse again, but found that he couldn't say the words.

"On behalf of this Christian congregation we say to you, 'Go on teaching the Word of God as you have for 20 years.'"

William couldn't hold out any longer. "Yes, my dear friends, oh, yes, I will do as you ask." ■

116

16

The New Metlakatla

William lived in the house the Indians had provided for him and continued teaching and counseling them. As much as possible he avoided going into the Mission House or having any conversations with Bishop Ridley. When the bishop left for England on business, William relaxed. He felt as if the constant cloud over his head had lifted.

Two weeks before the bishop was due back in Metlakatla, William received two letters. One was from Bishop Ridley. He had written that the church officials in England were very upset when they heard about the rift between himself and William.

In a roundabout way the bishop suggested that they start mending that rift. He seemed to want William to start sharing with him the duties and responsibilities of running Metlakatla.

William didn't like the way the letter was worded. The bishop seemed to be extending peace feelers, but said nothing definite about listening to William's views on things. William could see the possibility of the Indians being used as pawns in a constant struggle for control. He could see them becoming aware of the differences of opinion between two white men, both of whom were members of the same church.

He knew that such a situation could lead only to confusion and quarreling among the Indians themselves. If someone wasn't satisfied, that person could easily be influenced to take sides in the conflict and could be used to spread dissension among the others.

I don't want that, thought William, as he slowly tore open the second letter. As he read it, the words suddenly explained the reason why the bishop had written to him. It was from the Missionary Society in England and stated that William's letter explaining why he couldn't make the trip to England had been received and accepted. It also said that Bishop Ridley had been instructed to hurry back to Metlakatla and mend the rift between them as quickly as possible.

"He has been severely reprimanded for his hasty action," it concluded. "Everything possible must be done to bring the whole of Metlakatla back into the fold of the church."

When the bishop returned, William flatly turned down all his offers of reconciliation. All the while he was telling himself that perhaps he was just being stubborn, that he was trying to hang onto his pride. A few times he almost talked himself into compromising. Then he would see the bishop flaunting his regal robes as he strode through the village, or he would see the confusion in the Indians' eyes as the church services became more and more ornate and complicated.

No, he thought, I cannot be a part of this.

William knew that eventually there would be an open rupture within the community. The bishop had started telling the Indians that he was their rightful ruler and that only he had the backing of the Missionary Society.

118

"The Society has money which it can give to Metlakatla," he said to them. "Mr. Duncan is keeping you from your rightful share of that money."

William fumed but kept silent. He knew that the Indians wanted to be independent and take care of themselves. The village council sent two letters to the bishop, asking him to leave. He tore them both up.

The bishop had a series of confrontations with individual Indians. A native with a sense of humor came up to him and grabbed both of his hands. He raised one hand and called out, "This hand baptize Indian!"

Then he raised the other hand. "And this hand fight Indian!"

The bishop scuffled with him for a moment as 20 or 30 Indians gathered around to watch. The entire incident was over within a few minutes.

The next day a warship arrived. Bishop Ridley had reported that 250 natives had started a riot and had attacked him.

It was becoming harder and harder for William to control his anger. Most of the natives understood what was happening and flocked to William's side. The bishop, however, was slowly undermining his authority with many of them. A few of the chiefs who had continued to harbor resentment because of their lost power and others whom William had had to discipline listened to the bishop's words eagerly.

William's biggest concern was that the strife would undermine the Indians' faith in Christianity. When Bishop Ridley appeared one day carrying a rifle and looking carefully at every group of natives, his concern sharpened. After all, the natives were only one step away from a life of violence themselves. To see a white man—a leader of the church—carrying a weapon could be devastating to them.

The last straw came when Bishop Ridley aligned himself with the land speculators who were again trying to seize the ancestral lands of the Tsimshians. At that point William decided to go to Ottawa to plead the Indians' cause with the Dominion government. Sir John MacDonald, the Premier, listened gravely, then promised his support, on the condition that William himself would serve as the local superintendent of Indian affairs.

"I would be happy to serve," William said, "but I shall refuse to accept a salary for the position."

Sir John told William that it would take six months to pass the necessary laws and put them into action. Satisfied that the Tsimshians would at least be able to remain at Metlakatla instead of being herded onto a reservation, William decided to wait out the six months in England. The situation at the village was so unstable that he knew his presence might start an uprising.

William waited six months. No word came from Sir John about saving the Indians' land. Two more months passed with no word. By this time William knew something must have happened to change Sir John's mind. He wrote several carefully worded letters, which were never answered.

Something told him that he had better hurry back to Metlakatla. When he arrived, he was aghast at what he discovered. A surveying party had already been sent from Ottawa and was parceling out a section of land for the establishment of a reservation. The area was only a fraction of what rightfully belonged to the Tsimshians.

The Indians had been desperately trying some delaying tactics. As fast as the surveyors drove in the stakes marking the borders, the Indians pulled them up. When they put up a chain, the Indians saw that it was removed.

An Indian put up a small building on part of the land the government was claiming. When he claimed possession of the land and the building, the bishop swore out an injunction against him. The next day a warship arrived. Bishop Ridley had asked for help in getting what he wanted.

William immediately went to Victoria for one last effort to stop the seizure of the land. A final ruling was handed down: "The Indians have no rights in the land except such as might be accorded them by the bounty and charity of the Queen of England."

William felt more discouraged and beaten than he had ever felt in his life. Once again the white man, not the Indian, had come between him and his dream of a Christian community.

Before he left the city, he expressed his feelings to one of the secretaries who had told William he thought the Indians were being cheated.

"May God have mercy on the people of this province," William said. "Your population will be murdered by the Indians. I have pleaded and preached and prayed about the injustices that have been showered on these poor Indians."

"It is terrible to contemplate," agreed the secretary, "but we have deserved it. I admit it. I admit it."

On the way back to Metlakatla a small idea started growing in William's head. By the time he arrived at the village he was bursting with his new plan. He could hardly wait to talk to some of the Indian leaders in private. When he had gathered a group of them in his house, he paused for a moment of silent prayer before he spoke. He wasn't at all sure how the Tsimshians would feel about his idea. He started to speak, choosing his words carefully.

When he was through, he shut his eyes, not wanting to look at the faces of his friends. If they showed disapproval, he didn't want to see it.

Finally one of them broke the silence. "Yes, it is good. We should move our people to Alaska. We do not want to stay here and be slaves. We do not want to kill. A Christian can suffer. He can die. But he cannot kill. Let us go to the land of the free. We are slaves here. There we can be free men. We love this land, but we love Christ more."

Tears poured out of William's eyes, and he couldn't speak over the lump in his throat. God's love had won out over the governments of men and the hypocrisy which existed within the church. He was sure that the Indians knew that the move would be a difficult one, but if they worked together they could build a new life once more.

Civic and church leaders in the United States welcomed the villagers of Metlakatla with open arms. Everything was quickly arranged so they could make their new home on the Alaskan archipelago. On March 25, 1887, the new Metlakatla was founded at Port Chester on Annette Island.

William arrived on the steamer on Aug. 7. Temporary cabins had been erected by the Indians who had gone ahead. William gazed at the waterfall and envisioned a new sawmill. He saw the sheltered bay and pictured the steamer being loaded with goods to sell along the coast. The fine beaches would soon be lined with canoes filled with fish. The gently rising stretch of land and the luxurious growth of cedar, spruce, and hemlock provided the setting for the scene which was rapidly taking shape in William's imagination.

Soon after he landed, a temporary flagpole had been rigged up. The Stars and Stripes was raised to the accompaniment of a cannon's roar. Several American officials joined in the cheers of Metlakatla's citizens.

Within a few days almost the entire population of the old village had moved their belongings to the new site. Only 100 of the original 950 people chose to stay with Bishop Ridley. Most of the ones who remained were too old to start life over again in a new land.

Men, women, and children went right to work to rebuild their village. Interested people throughout the United States heard of the struggling Indians, and within two years thousands of dollars had been contributed toward the rebuilding. In January 1889 William was able to write:

> Christmas and New Year's is always a joyous season with the people of Metlakatla, and the last one has proved to be no exception to the rule. Though still living in temporary shanties, built among the stumps and huge trees, both standing and fallen, yet the people are healthy and happy. . . . Smiling faces greet you everywhere, and the village storekeepers are overwhelmed with business.

One day a few months later a visitor was talking to William. "I am so impressed by what you have done," she remarked. "What have you done about a successor? What is to become of this glorious work when you die?"

William did not speak. Instead, he simply lifted his right hand and pointed toward the sky. He knew that God would provide for Metlakatla long after he himself climbed that great ladder into heaven.■